Microsoft®
Excel 2000
Simplified™

IDG's **3-D Visual**™ Series

IDG BOOKS *From* **maranGraphics**™

IDG Books Worldwide, Inc.
An International Data Group Company
Foster City, CA • Indianapolis • Chicago • New York

Microsoft® Excel 2000 Simplified™

Published by
IDG Books Worldwide, Inc.
An International Data Group Company
919 E. Hillsdale Blvd., Suite 400
Foster City, CA 94404
(650) 655-3000

Copyright© 1999 by maranGraphics Inc.
5755 Coopers Avenue
Mississauga, Ontario, Canada
L4Z 1R9

Library of Congress Catalog Card No.: 99-62445
ISBN: 0-7645-6053-0
Printed in the United States of America
10 9 8 7 6 5 4 3 2 1

Distributed in the United States by IDG Books Worldwide, Inc.
Distributed by CDG Books Canada Inc. for Canada; by Transworld Publishers Limited in the United Kingdom; by IDG Norge Books for Norway; by IDG Sweden Books for Sweden; by Woodslane Pty. Ltd. for Australia; by Woodslane (NZ) Ltd. for New Zealand; by TransQuest Publishers Pte Ltd. for Singapore, Malaysia, Thailand, Indonesia, and Hong Kong; by ICG Muse, Inc. for Japan; by Norma Comunicaciones S.A. for Colombia; by Intersoft for South Africa; by Le Monde en Tique for France; by International Thomson Publishing for Germany, Austria and Switzerland; by Distribuidora Cuspide for Argentina; by Livraria Cultura for Brazil; by Ediciones ZETA S.C.R. Ltda. for Peru; by WS Computer Publishing Corporation, Inc., for the Philippines; by Contemporanea de Ediciones for Venezuela; by Express Computer Distributors for the Caribbean and West Indies; by Micronesia Media Distributor, Inc. for Micronesia; by Grupo Editorial Norma S.A. for Guatemala; by Chips Computadoras S.A. de C.V. for Mexico; by Editorial Norma de Panama S.A. for Panama; by American Bookshops for Finland. Authorized Sales Agent: Anthony Rudkin Associates for the Middle East and North Africa.
For corporate orders, please call maranGraphics at 800-469-6616.
For general information on IDG Books Worldwide's books in the U.S., please call our Consumer Customer Service department at 800-762-2974.
For reseller information, including discounts and premium sales, please call our Reseller Customer Service department at 800-434-3422.
For information on where to purchase IDG Books Worldwide's books outside the U.S., please contact our International Sales department at 317-596-5530 or fax 317-596-5692.
For consumer information on foreign language translations, please contact our Customer Service department at 1-800-434-3422, fax 317-596-5692, or e-mail rights@idgbooks.com.
For information on licensing foreign or domestic rights, please phone 1-650-655-3109.
For sales inquiries and special prices for bulk quantities, please contact our Sales department at 650-655-3200.
For information on using IDG Books Worldwide's books in the classroom or for ordering examination copies, please contact our Educational Sales department at 800-434-2086 or fax 317-596-5499.
For press review copies, author interviews, or other publicity information, please contact our Public Relations department at 650-655-3000 or fax 650-655-3299.
For authorization to photocopy items for corporate, personal, or educational use, please contact maranGraphics at 800-469-6616.

Trademark Acknowledgments

Permissions

©1999
maranGraphics, Inc.

The 3-D illustrations are the copyright of maranGraphics, Inc.

U.S. Corporate Sales	**U.S. Trade Sales**
Contact maranGraphics at (800) 469-6616 or fax (905) 890-9434.	Contact IDG Books at (800) 434-3422 or (650) 655-3000.

ABOUT IDG BOOKS WORLDWIDE

Welcome to the world of IDG Books Worldwide.

IDG Books Worldwide, Inc., is a subsidiary of International Data Group, the world's largest publisher of computer-related information and the leading global provider of information services on information technology. IDG was founded more than 30 years ago by Patrick J. McGovern and now employs more than 9,000 people worldwide. IDG publishes more than 290 computer publications in over 75 countries. More than 90 million people read one or more IDG publications each month.

Launched in 1990, IDG Books Worldwide is today the #1 publisher of best-selling computer books in the United States. We are proud to have received eight awards from the Computer Press Association in recognition of editorial excellence and three from Computer Currents' First Annual Readers' Choice Awards. Our best-selling *...For Dummies®* series has more than 50 million copies in print with translations in 31 languages. IDG Books Worldwide, through a joint venture with IDG's Hi-Tech Beijing, became the first U.S. publisher to publish a computer book in the People's Republic of China. In record time, IDG Books Worldwide has become the first choice for millions of readers around the world who want to learn how to better manage their businesses.

Our mission is simple: Every one of our books is designed to bring extra value and skill-building instructions to the reader. Our books are written by experts who understand and care about our readers. The knowledge base of our editorial staff comes from years of experience in publishing, education, and journalism — experience we use to produce books to carry us into the new millennium. In short, we care about books, so we attract the best people. We devote special attention to details such as audience, interior design, use of icons, and illustrations. And because we use an efficient process of authoring, editing, and desktop publishing our books electronically, we can spend more time ensuring superior content and less time on the technicalities of making books.

You can count on our commitment to deliver high-quality books at competitive prices on topics you want to read about. At IDG Books Worldwide, we continue in the IDG tradition of delivering quality for more than 30 years. You'll find no better book on a subject than one from IDG Books Worldwide.

John Kilcullen
Chairman and CEO
IDG Books Worldwide, Inc.

Steven Berkowitz
President and Publisher
IDG Books Worldwide, Inc.

VIII WINNER
Eighth Annual
Computer Press
Awards ≥1992

IX WINNER
Ninth Annual
Computer Press
Awards ≥1993

X WINNER
Tenth Annual
Computer Press
Awards ≥1994

XI WINNER
Eleventh Annual
Computer Press
Awards ≥1995

IDG is the world's leading IT media, research and exposition company. Founded in 1964, IDG had 1997 revenues of $2.05 billion and has more than 9,000 employees worldwide. IDG offers the widest range of media options that reach IT buyers in 75 countries representing 95% of worldwide IT spending. IDG's diverse product and services portfolio spans six key areas including print publishing, online publishing, expositions and conferences, market research, education and training, and global marketing services. More than 90 million people read one or more of IDG's 290 magazines and newspapers, including IDG's leading global brands — Computerworld, PC World, Network World, Macworld and the Channel World family of publications. IDG Books Worldwide is one of the fastest-growing computer book publishers in the world, with more than 700 titles in 36 languages. The "...For Dummies®" series alone has more than 50 million copies in print. IDG offers online users the largest network of technology-specific Web sites around the world through IDG.net (http://www.idg.net), which comprises more than 225 targeted Web sites in 55 countries worldwide. International Data Corporation (IDC) is the world's largest provider of information technology data, analysis and consulting, with research centers in over 41 countries and more than 400 research analysts worldwide. IDG World Expo is a leading producer of more than 168 globally branded conferences and expositions in 35 countries including E3 (Electronic Entertainment Expo), Macworld Expo, ComNet, Windows World Expo, ICE (Internet Commerce Expo), Agenda, DEMO, and Spotlight. IDG's training subsidiary, ExecuTrain, is the world's largest computer training company, with more than 230 locations worldwide and 785 training courses. IDG Marketing Services helps industry-leading IT companies build international brand recognition by developing global integrated marketing programs via IDG's print, online and exposition products worldwide. Further information about the company can be found at www.idg.com.   1/24/99

maranGraphics is a family-run business located near Toronto, Canada.

At **maranGraphics**, we believe in producing great computer books—one book at a time.

Each maranGraphics book uses the award-winning communication process that we have been developing over the last 25 years. Using this process, we organize screen shots, text and illustrations in a way that makes it easy for you to learn new concepts and tasks.

We spend hours deciding the best way to perform each task, so you don't have to! Our clear, easy-to-follow screen shots and instructions walk you through each task from beginning to end.

Our detailed illustrations go hand-in-hand with the text to help reinforce the information. Each illustration is a labor of love—some take up to a week to draw!

We want to thank you for purchasing what we feel are the best computer books money can buy. We hope you enjoy using this book as much as we enjoyed creating it!

Sincerely,

The Maran Family

Please visit us on the web at:
www.maran.com

Credits

Authors:
Ruth Maran
Kelleigh Wing

Copy Editors:
Roxanne Van Damme
Jill Maran

Project Manager:
Judy Maran

Editing & Screen Captures:
Raquel Scott
Janice Boyer
Michelle Kirchner
James Menzies
Frances Lea
Emmet Mellow

Layout Designers:
Treena Lees
Jamie Bell

Illustrators:
Russ Marini
Jamie Bell
Peter Grecco
Sean Johannesen
Steven Schaerer

Screen Artist & Corrections:
Jimmy Tam

Indexer:
Raquel Scott

Post Production:
Robert Maran

Editorial Support:
Michael Roney

Acknowledgments

Thanks to the dedicated staff of maranGraphics, including
Jamie Bell, Cathy Benn, Janice Boyer, Francisco Ferreira,
Peter Grecco, Jenn Hillman, Sean Johannesen, Michelle Kirchner,
Wanda Lawrie, Frances Lea, Treena Lees, Jill Maran, Judy Maran,
Maxine Maran, Robert Maran, Sherry Maran, Russ Marini,
Emmet Mellow, James Menzies, Steven Schaerer, Raquel Scott,
Jimmy Tam, Roxanne Van Damme and Paul Whitehead.

Finally, to Richard Maran who originated the easy-to-use
graphic format of this guide. Thank you for your
inspiration and guidance.

Table of Contents

CHAPTER 1

GETTING STARTED

Introduction to Excel 4

Using the Mouse 6

Start Excel 7

The Excel Screen 8

Change the Active Cell 9

Enter Data 10

Select Cells 12

Complete a Series 14

Scroll Through a Worksheet 16

Select Commands Using Menus 18

Select Commands Using Toolbars 20

Display or Hide a Toolbar 21

Size a Toolbar 22

Move a Toolbar 23

Getting Help 24

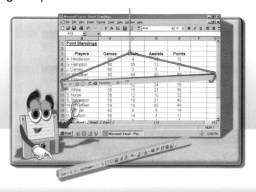

CHAPTER 2

SAVE AND OPEN YOUR WORKBOOKS

Save a Workbook 28

Create a New Workbook 30

Switch Between Workbooks 31

Close a Workbook 32

Exit Excel 33

Open a Workbook 34

Find a Workbook 36

CHAPTER 3

EDIT YOUR WORKSHEETS

Edit Data 42

Delete Data 44

Undo Changes 45

Move or Copy Data 46

Check Spelling .50

Find Data 52

Replace Data 54

Insert a Row or Column 56

Delete a Row or Column 58

Name Cells 60

CHAPTER 4

WORK WITH FORMULAS AND FUNCTIONS

Introduction to Formulas 64

Enter a Formula 66

Introduction to Functions 68

Enter a Function 70

Using AutoCalculate 74

Add Numbers .76

Copy a Formula 78

Errors in Formulas 82

CHAPTER 5

CHANGE YOUR SCREEN DISPLAY

Display Full Screen 86

Zoom In or Out 87

Hide Columns .88

Hide Rows 90

Freeze Rows and Columns 92

Split a Worksheet 94

CHAPTER 6

FORMAT YOUR WORKSHEETS

Change Column Width 98

Change Row Height 99

Change Font of Data 100

Change Size of Data 101

Bold, Italicize or Underline Data 102

Change Alignment of Data 103

Change Appearance of Data 104

Table of Contents

Change Cell or Data Color 108

Add Borders 110

Clear Formatting 111

Change Number Format 112

Indent Data 116

Center Data Across Columns 117

Wrap Text in Cells 118

Rotate Data in Cells 120

Copy Formatting 122

Apply an AutoFormat 124

CHAPTER 7

PRINT YOUR WORKSHEETS

Preview a Worksheet 128

Print a Worksheet 130

Set a Print Area 132

Center Data on a Page 134

Change Page Orientation 135

Change Margins 136

Change Print Options 138

Insert a Page Break 140

Add a Header or Footer 142

Change Size of Printed Data 144

Repeat Labels on Printed Pages 146

CHAPTER 8

WORK WITH MULTIPLE WORKSHEETS

Switch Between Worksheets 150

Insert a Worksheet 152

Delete a Worksheet 153

Rename a Worksheet 154

Move a Worksheet 155

Move or Copy Data Between Worksheets . . .156

Enter a Formula Across Worksheets 158

CHAPTER 9

WORK WITH CHARTS

Introduction to Charts 162

Create a Chart 164

Move or Size a Chart 168

Print a Chart 170

Change Chart Type 172

Change Chart Titles 174

Change the Way Data is Plotted 175

Add Data to a Chart 176

CHAPTER 10

WORK WITH GRAPHICS

Add an AutoShape 180

Add a Text Effect 182

Add a Text Box 184

Move or Size a Graphic 186

Change Color of a Graphic 188

Make a Graphic 3-D 189

CHAPTER 11

MANAGE DATA IN A LIST

Create a List 192

Sort Data in a List 194

Filter a List 198

Add Subtotals to a List 202

CHAPTER 12

EXCEL AND THE INTERNET

E-mail a Worksheet 208

Create a Hyperlink 210

Preview a Workbook as a Web Page 214

Save a Workbook as a Web Page 216

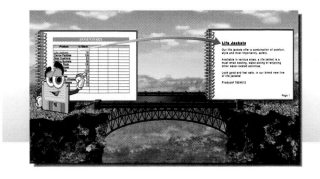

CHAPTER 1

GETTING STARTED

Are you ready to begin using Microsoft Excel 2000? This chapter will help you get started.

Introduction to Excel 4

Using the Mouse 6

Start Excel .7

The Excel Screen 8

Change the Active Cell 9

Enter Data .10

Select Cells .12

Complete a Series 14

Scroll Through a Worksheet 16

Select Commands Using Menus 18

Select Commands Using Toolbars 20

Display or Hide a Toolbar 21

Size a Toolbar 22

Move a Toolbar 23

Getting Help .24

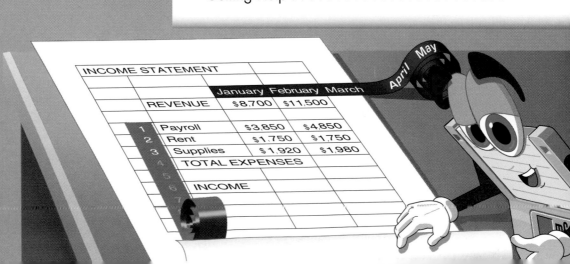

Excel is a spreadsheet program you can use to organize, analyze and attractively present data such as a budget or sales report.

Enter and Edit Data

Excel lets you efficiently enter and edit data in a worksheet. Excel can help you quickly enter data by completing a series of numbers for you. You can add, delete or move data to a new location.

You can also check a worksheet for spelling errors and instantly undo changes you regret.

Use Formulas and Functions

Formulas and functions allow you to perform calculations and analyze data in a worksheet. Common calculations include finding the sum, average or total number of items in a list.

Format Worksheets

Excel includes many formatting features that can help you change the appearance of a worksheet. You can add borders, change the color of cells, use various fonts and change the alignment of data.

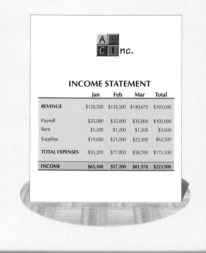

Print Worksheets

You can produce a paper copy of a worksheet you create. Before printing, you can see on your screen how the worksheet will look when printed. You can adjust the margins or change the orientation of the printed data.

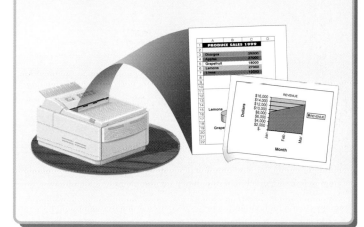

Create Charts and Graphics

Excel helps you create colorful charts from worksheet data to visually display the data. You can also create graphics, such as AutoShapes, text effects and text boxes, to enhance the appearance of a worksheet and illustrate important concepts.

Manage Data in a List

Excel provides tools that help you manage and analyze a large collection of data, such as a mailing list or product list. You can sort or filter the data in a list. You can also add subtotals to summarize the data.

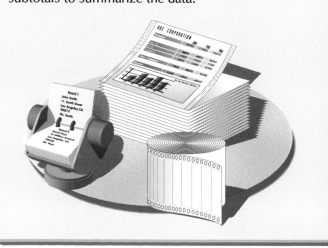

Excel and the Internet

You can save a workbook you create as a Web page. This lets you place the workbook on the Internet for other people to view. You can also add a hyperlink to a workbook to connect the workbook to a Web page.

A mouse is a handheld device that lets you select and move items on your screen.

When you move the mouse on your desk, the mouse pointer on your screen moves in the same direction. The mouse pointer assumes different shapes, such as ⬚ or ⬚, depending on its location on your screen and the task you are performing.

Resting your hand on the mouse, use your thumb and two rightmost fingers to move the mouse on your desk. Use your two remaining fingers to press the mouse buttons.

MOUSE ACTIONS

Click

Press and release the left mouse button.

Double-click

Quickly press and release the left mouse button twice.

Right-click

Press and release the right mouse button.

Drag

Position the mouse pointer over an object on your screen and then press and hold down the left mouse button. Still holding down the button, move the mouse to where you want to place the object and then release the button.

When you start Excel, a blank worksheet appears on your screen. You can enter data into this worksheet.

START EXCEL

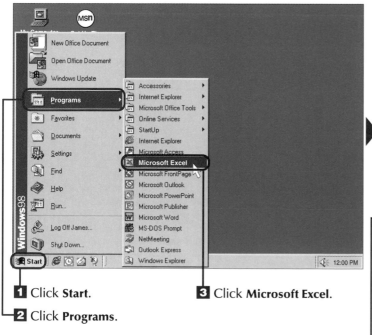

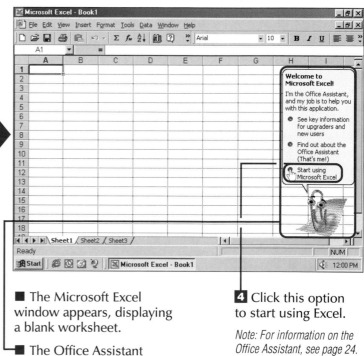

1 Click **Start**.

2 Click **Programs**.

3 Click **Microsoft Excel**.

■ The Microsoft Excel window appears, displaying a blank worksheet.

■ The Office Assistant welcome appears the first time you start Excel.

4 Click this option to start using Excel.

Note: For information on the Office Assistant, see page 24.

THE EXCEL SCREEN

The Excel screen displays several items to help you perform tasks efficiently.

Menu Bar

Provides access to lists of commands available in Excel.

Formatting Toolbar

Contains buttons to help you select common formatting commands, such as Bold and Underline.

Standard Toolbar

Contains buttons to help you select common commands, such as Save and Print.

Formula Bar

Displays the cell reference and contents of the active cell. A cell reference identifies the location of a cell in a worksheet and consists of a column letter followed by a row number, such as **A1**.

Active Cell

Displays a thick border. You enter data into the active cell.

Cell

The area where a row and column intersect.

Row

A horizontal line of cells. A number identifies each row.

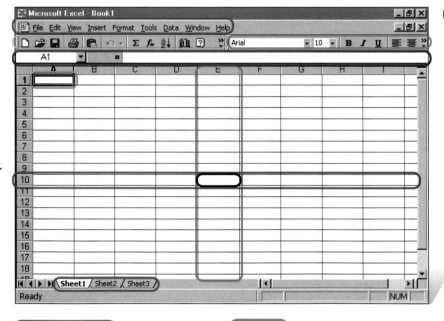

Worksheet Tabs

An Excel file is called a workbook. Each workbook is divided into several worksheets. Excel displays a tab for each worksheet.

A workbook is similar to a three-ring binder that contains several sheets of paper.

Column

A vertical line of cells. A letter identifies each column.

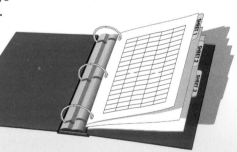

CHANGE THE ACTIVE CELL

You can make any cell in your worksheet the active cell. You enter data into the active cell.

CHANGE THE ACTIVE CELL

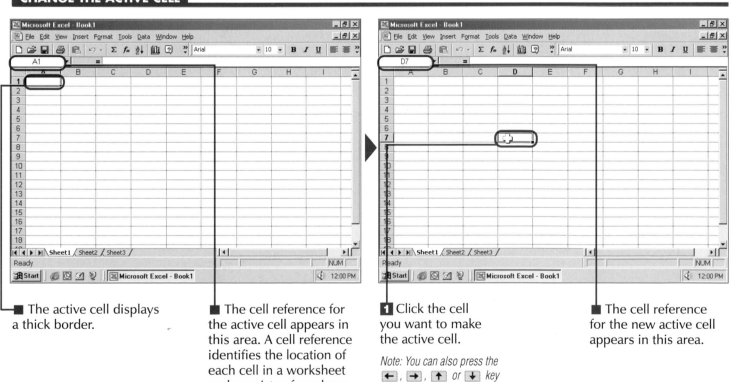

■ The active cell displays a thick border.

■ The cell reference for the active cell appears in this area. A cell reference identifies the location of each cell in a worksheet and consists of a column letter followed by a row number (example: **A1**).

1 Click the cell you want to make the active cell.

Note: You can also press the
←, →, ↑ or ↓ key
to change the active cell.

■ The cell reference for the new active cell appears in this area.

SALES REPORT IN UNITS

	1995	1996	1997	1998
January	10500	8850	9000	10400
February	9400	9750	9500	9850
March	6450	8450	8950	9900
April	7890	9000	9400	10850
May	8920	7359	8700	11500

You can enter data into your worksheet quickly and easily.

ENTER DATA

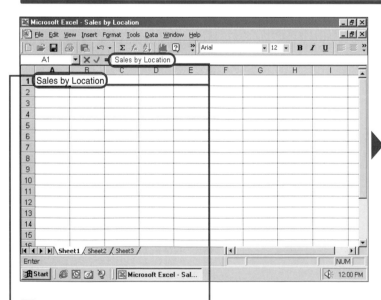

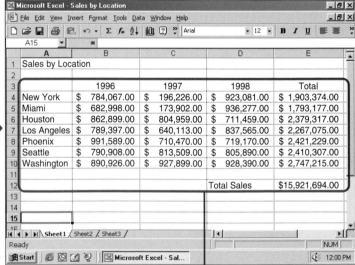

1 Click the cell where you want to enter data. Then type the data.

Note: In this example, the size of data was changed from 10 point to 12 point to make the data easier to read.

■ If you make a typing mistake, press the **+Backspace** key to remove the incorrect data. Then type the correct data.

■ The data you type appears in the active cell and the formula bar.

2 Press the **Enter** key to enter the data and move down one cell.

Note: To enter the data and move one cell in any direction, press the ←, →, ↑ or ↓ key.

3 Repeat steps **1** and **2** until you finish entering all your data.

Why did Excel change a number I entered?

If you type a number such as a zip code or product number, Excel may automatically change the appearance of the number. To have Excel display the number exactly as you enter it, type an apostrophe (') in front of the number. The apostrophe will not appear in your worksheet.

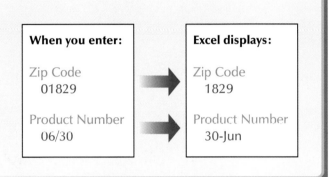

When you enter:	Excel displays:
Zip Code 01829	Zip Code 1829
Product Number 06/30	Product Number 30-Jun

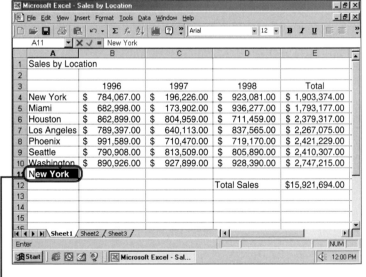

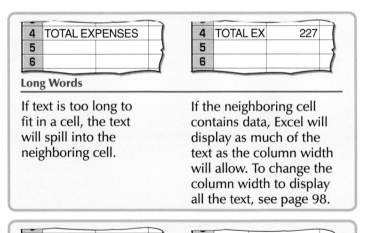

4	TOTAL EXPENSES
5	
6	

4	TOTAL EX	227
5	
6	

Long Words

If text is too long to fit in a cell, the text will spill into the neighboring cell.

If the neighboring cell contains data, Excel will display as much of the text as the column width will allow. To change the column width to display all the text, see page 98.

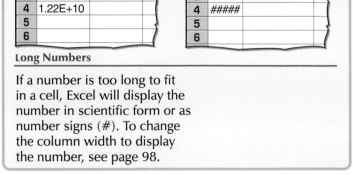

4	1.22E+10
5	
6	

4	#####
5	
6	

Long Numbers

If a number is too long to fit in a cell, Excel will display the number in scientific form or as number signs (#). To change the column width to display the number, see page 98.

AUTOCOMPLETE

■ If the first few letters you type match another cell in the column, Excel may complete the text for you.

1 To enter the text Excel provides, press the `Enter` key.

■ To enter different text, continue typing.

Before performing many tasks in Excel, you must select the cells you want to work with. Selected cells appear highlighted on your screen.

SELECT CELLS

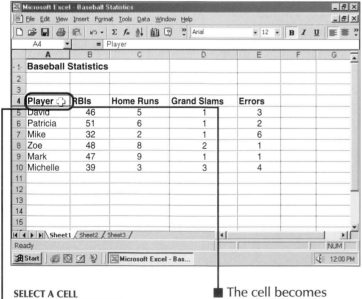

SELECT A CELL

1 Click the cell you want to select.

■ The cell becomes the active cell and displays a thick border.

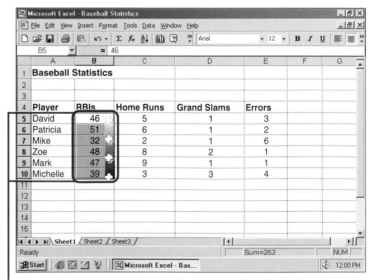

SELECT A GROUP OF CELLS

1 Position the mouse ⊹ over the first cell you want to select.

2 Drag the mouse ⊹ until you highlight all the cells you want to select.

■ To select multiple groups of cells, press and hold down the **Ctrl** key as you repeat steps **1** and **2** for each group.

■ To deselect cells, click any cell.

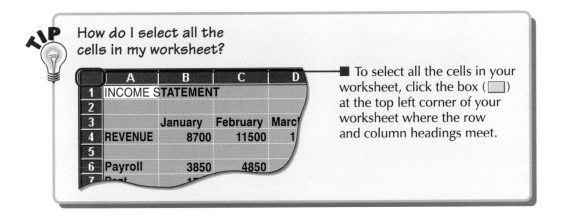

TIP

How do I select all the cells in my worksheet?

■ To select all the cells in your worksheet, click the box (⬜) at the top left corner of your worksheet where the row and column headings meet.

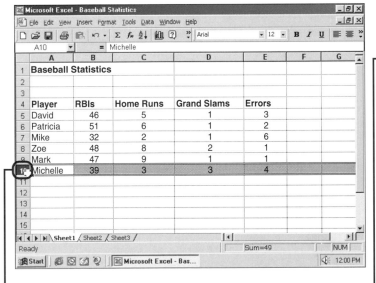

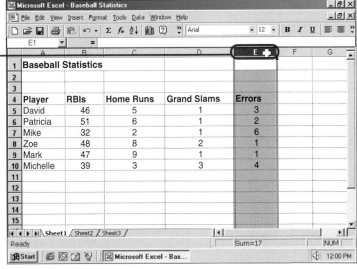

SELECT A ROW

1 Click the number of the row you want to select.

■ To select multiple rows, position the mouse ⊹ over the number of the first row you want to select. Then drag the mouse ⊹ until you highlight all the rows you want to select.

SELECT A COLUMN

1 Click the letter of the column you want to select.

■ To select multiple columns, position the mouse ⊹ over the letter of the first column you want to select. Then drag the mouse ⊹ until you highlight all the columns you want to select.

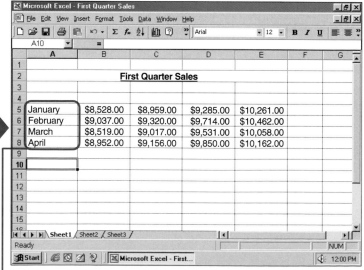

Excel can save you time by completing a text or number series for you.

You can complete a series across a row or down a column in a worksheet.

COMPLETE A TEXT SERIES

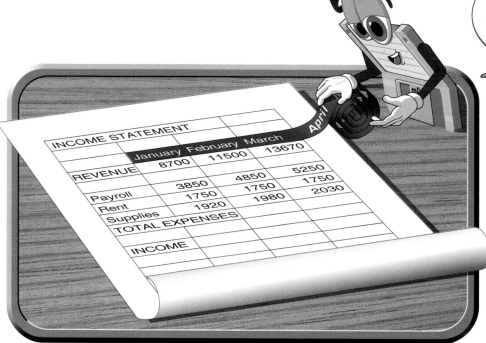

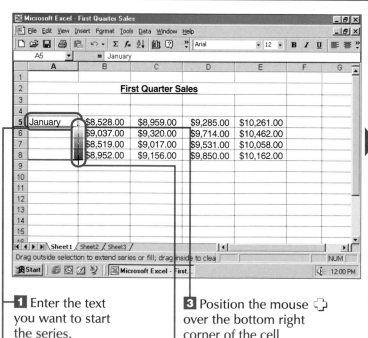

1 Enter the text you want to start the series.

2 Click the cell containing the text you entered.

3 Position the mouse ⊹ over the bottom right corner of the cell (⊹ changes to +).

4 Drag the mouse + over the cells you want to include in the series.

■ The cells display the text series.

Note: If Excel cannot determine the text series you want to complete, it will copy the text in the first cell to the cells you select.

■ To deselect cells, click any cell.

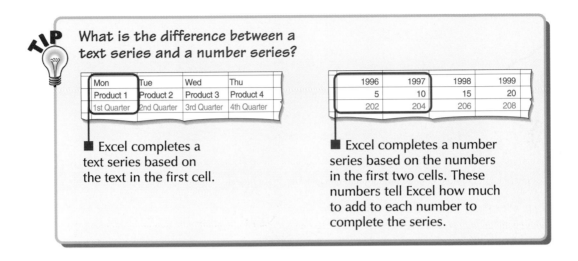

TIP

What is the difference between a text series and a number series?

Mon	Tue	Wed	Thu
Product 1	Product 2	Product 3	Product 4
1st Quarter	2nd Quarter	3rd Quarter	4th Quarter

1996	1997	1998	1999
5	10	15	20
202	204	206	208

■ Excel completes a text series based on the text in the first cell.

■ Excel completes a number series based on the numbers in the first two cells. These numbers tell Excel how much to add to each number to complete the series.

COMPLETE A NUMBER SERIES

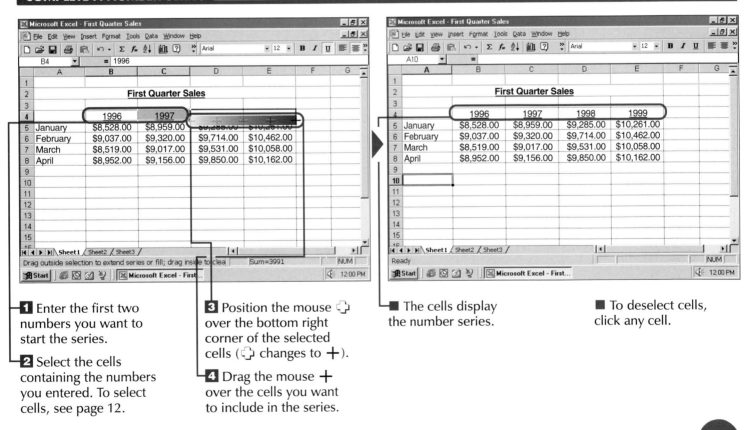

1 Enter the first two numbers you want to start the series.

2 Select the cells containing the numbers you entered. To select cells, see page 12.

3 Position the mouse ⬚ over the bottom right corner of the selected cells (⬚ changes to ✛).

4 Drag the mouse ✛ over the cells you want to include in the series.

■ The cells display the number series.

■ To deselect cells, click any cell.

SCROLL THROUGH A WORKSHEET

If your worksheet contains a lot of data, your computer screen may not be able to display all the data at once. You must scroll through your worksheet to view other areas of the worksheet.

SCROLL THROUGH A WORKSHEET

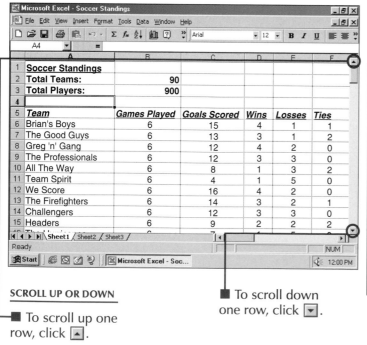

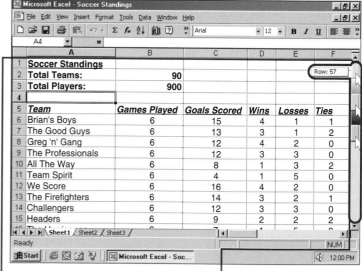

SCROLL UP OR DOWN

■ To scroll up one row, click ▲.

■ To scroll down one row, click ▼.

1 To quickly scroll to any row in the worksheet, position the mouse ⟍ over the scroll box.

2 Drag the scroll box along the scroll bar until a yellow box displays the number of the row you want to appear at the top of the worksheet.

TIP

How do I use a wheeled mouse to scroll through my worksheet?

A wheeled mouse has a wheel between the left and right mouse buttons. Moving this wheel lets you quickly scroll through your worksheet. The Microsoft IntelliMouse is a popular example of a wheeled mouse.

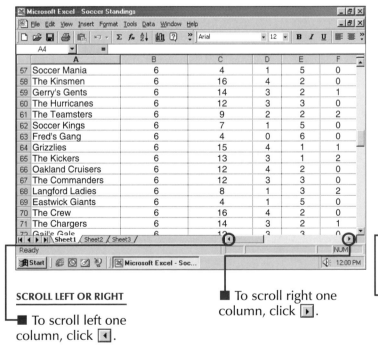

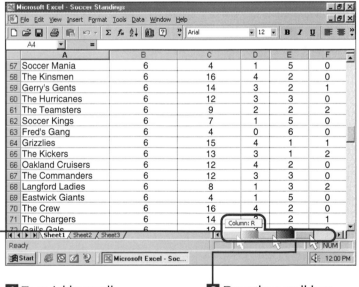

SCROLL LEFT OR RIGHT

■ To scroll left one column, click ◄.

■ To scroll right one column, click ►.

1 To quickly scroll to any column in the worksheet, position the mouse ☐ over the scroll box.

2 Drag the scroll box along the scroll bar until a yellow box displays the letter of the column you want to appear at the left side of the worksheet.

SELECT COMMANDS USING MENUS

You can select a command from a menu to perform a task. Each command performs a different task.

SELECT COMMANDS USING MENUS

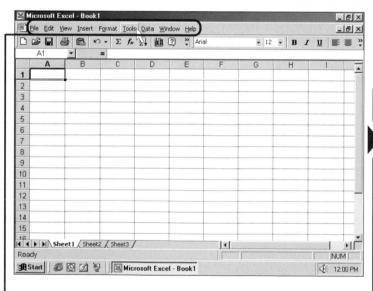

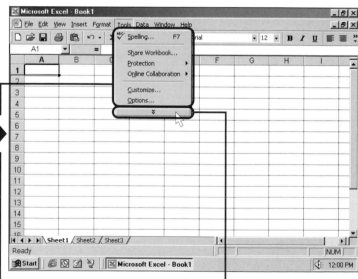

1 Click the name of the menu you want to display.

■ A short version of the menu appears, displaying the most commonly used commands.

2 To expand the menu and display all the commands, position the mouse ⟨ over ⤓.

Note: If you do not perform step 2, the expanded menu will automatically appear after a few seconds.

How can I make a command appear on the short version of a menu?

When you select a command from an expanded menu, the command is automatically added to the short version of the menu. The next time you display the short version of the menu, the command you selected will appear.

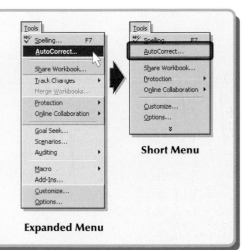

Short Menu

Expanded Menu

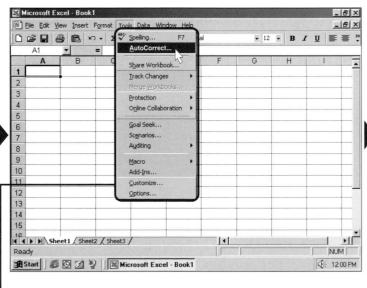

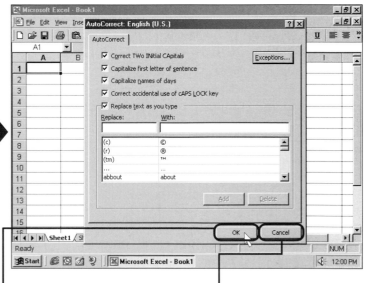

■ The expanded menu appears, displaying all the commands.

3 Click the command you want to use.

Note: A dimmed command is currently not available.

■ To close a menu without selecting a command, click outside the menu.

■ A dialog box appears if the command you selected displays three dots (...).

4 When you finish selecting options in the dialog box, click **OK** to confirm your changes.

■ To close the dialog box without selecting any options, click **Cancel**.

A toolbar contains buttons that you can use to select commands.

TOOLBARS

When you first start Excel, the most commonly used buttons appear on each toolbar. As you work with Excel, the toolbars automatically change to remove buttons you rarely use and display the buttons you use most often.

SELECT COMMANDS USING TOOLBARS

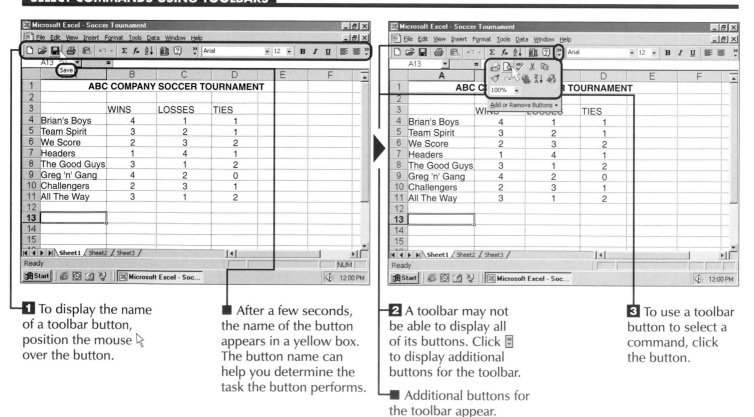

1 To display the name of a toolbar button, position the mouse � over the button.

■ After a few seconds, the name of the button appears in a yellow box. The button name can help you determine the task the button performs.

2 A toolbar may not be able to display all of its buttons. Click ⁑ to display additional buttons for the toolbar.

■ Additional buttons for the toolbar appear.

3 To use a toolbar button to select a command, click the button.

DISPLAY OR HIDE A TOOLBAR

Excel offers several toolbars that you can display or hide at any time. Each toolbar contains buttons that help you quickly perform common tasks.

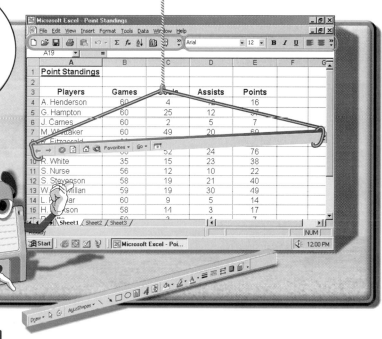

When you first start Excel, the Standard and Formatting toolbars appear on your screen.

Standard

Formatting

DISPLAY OR HIDE A TOOLBAR

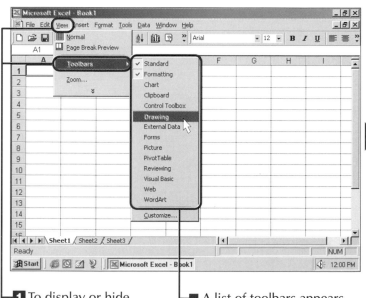

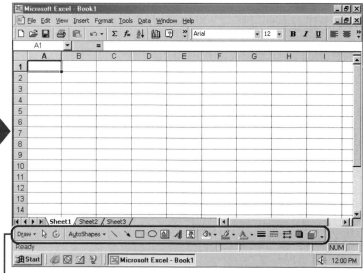

1 To display or hide a toolbar, click **View**.

2 Click **Toolbars**.

■ A list of toolbars appears. A check mark (✔) beside a toolbar name tells you the toolbar is currently displayed.

3 Click the name of the toolbar you want to display or hide.

■ Excel displays or hides the toolbar you selected.

You can increase the size of a toolbar to display more buttons on the toolbar. This is useful when a toolbar appears on the same row as another toolbar and cannot display all of its buttons.

You cannot size a toolbar that appears on its own row.

SIZE A TOOLBAR

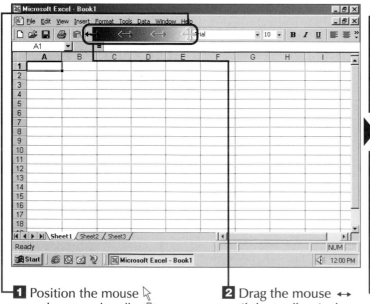

1 Position the mouse ⬡ over the move handle (▯) of the toolbar you want to size (⬡ changes to ✛).

2 Drag the mouse ↔ until the toolbar is the size you want.

■ The toolbar displays the new size.

■ The new toolbar size affects the location and size of other toolbars on the same row.

MOVE A TOOLBAR

You can move a toolbar to the top, bottom, right or left edge of your screen.

Moving a toolbar to its own row allows you to display more buttons on the toolbar.

MOVE A TOOLBAR

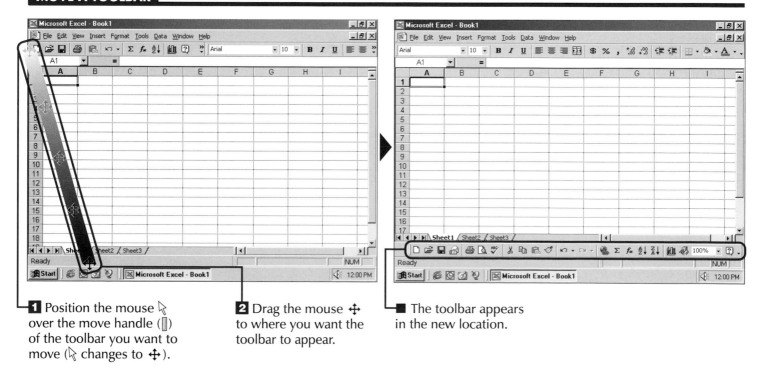

1 Position the mouse ⌖ over the move handle (▯) of the toolbar you want to move (⌖ changes to ✛).

2 Drag the mouse ✛ to where you want the toolbar to appear.

■ The toolbar appears in the new location.

23

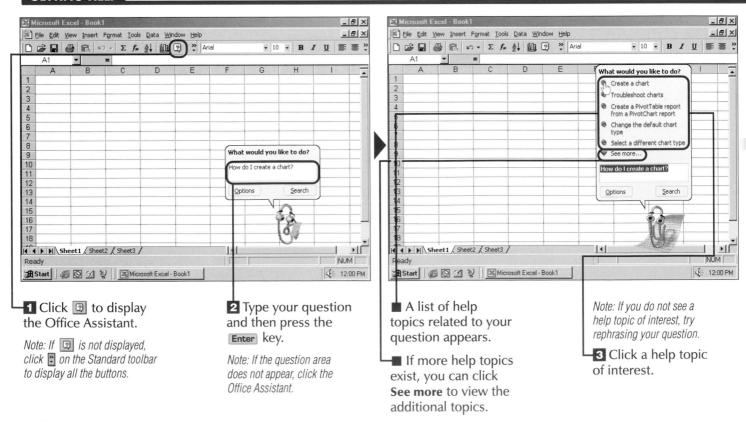

1 Click 🛄 to display the Office Assistant.

Note: If 🛄 is not displayed, click ⨠ on the Standard toolbar to display all the buttons.

2 Type your question and then press the `Enter` key.

Note: If the question area does not appear, click the Office Assistant.

■ A list of help topics related to your question appears.

■ If more help topics exist, you can click **See more** to view the additional topics.

Note: If you do not see a help topic of interest, try rephrasing your question.

3 Click a help topic of interest.

24

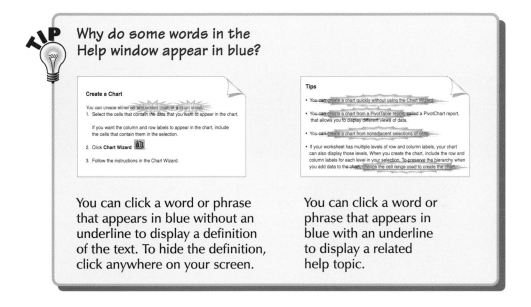

Why do some words in the Help window appear in blue?

You can click a word or phrase that appears in blue without an underline to display a definition of the text. To hide the definition, click anywhere on your screen.

You can click a word or phrase that appears in blue with an underline to display a related help topic.

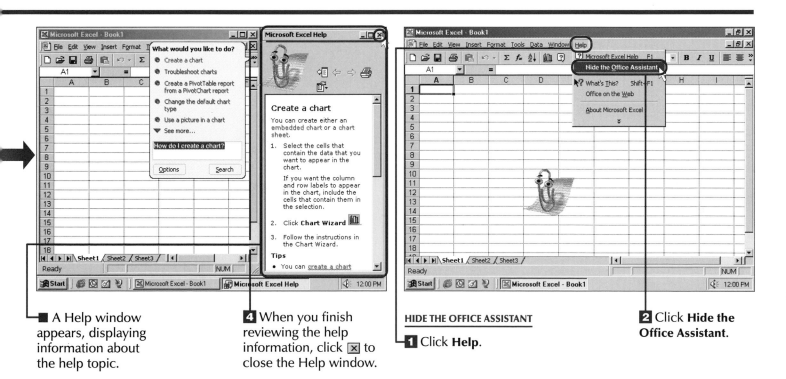

■ A Help window appears, displaying information about the help topic.

4 When you finish reviewing the help information, click ☒ to close the Help window.

HIDE THE OFFICE ASSISTANT

1 Click **Help**.

2 Click **Hide the Office Assistant**.

CHAPTER 2

SAVE AND OPEN YOUR WORKBOOKS

Are you wondering how to save, close or open an Excel workbook? Learn how in this chapter.

Save a Workbook 28

Create a New Workbook 30

Switch Between Workbooks 31

Close a Workbook 32

Exit Excel 33

Open a Workbook 34

Find a Workbook 36

You can save your workbook to store it for future use. This allows you to later review and make changes to the workbook.

SAVE A WORKBOOK

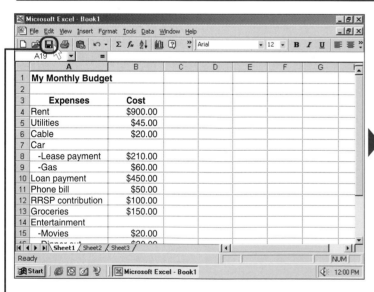

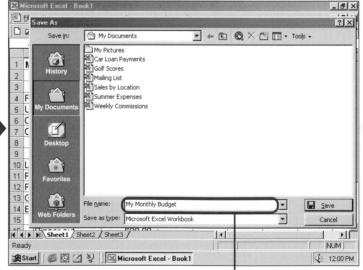

1 Click 🔲 to save your workbook.

Note: If 🔲 is not displayed, click ➡ on the Standard toolbar to display all the buttons.

■ The Save As dialog box appears.

Note: If you previously saved your workbook, the Save As dialog box will not appear since you have already named the workbook.

2 Type a name for the workbook.

What are the commonly used folders I can access?

History

Provides access to folders and workbooks you recently used.

My Documents

Provides a convenient place to store a workbook.

Desktop

Lets you store a workbook on the Windows desktop.

Favorites

Provides a place to store a workbook you will frequently access.

Web Folders

Can help you store a workbook on the Web.

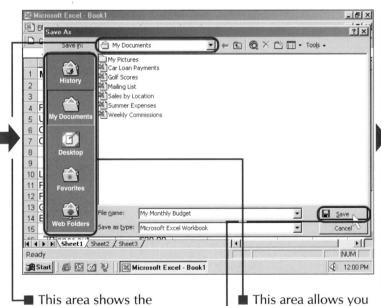

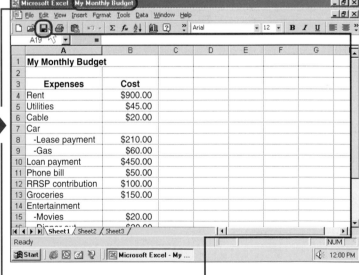

■ This area shows the location where Excel will store your workbook. You can click this area to change the location.

■ This area allows you to access commonly used folders. To display the contents of a folder, click the folder.

3 Click **Save**.

■ Excel saves your workbook and displays the name of the workbook at the top of your screen.

You should regularly save changes you make to a workbook to avoid losing your work.

1 Click 🖫 to save changes you make to your workbook.

CREATE A NEW WORKBOOK

You can easily create another workbook to store new data.

CREATE A NEW WORKBOOK

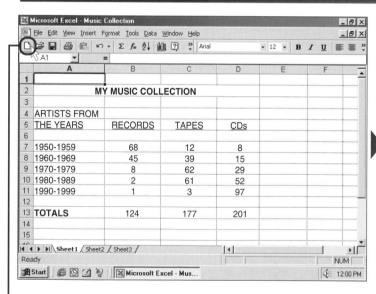

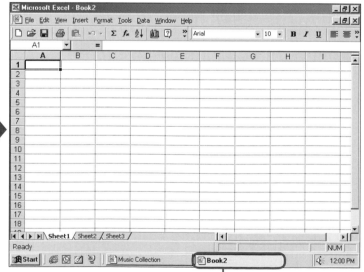

1 Click 🗋 to create a new workbook.

Note: If 🗋 is not displayed, click ⨠ on the Standard toolbar to display all the buttons.

■ A new workbook appears. The previous workbook is now hidden behind the new workbook.

■ A button for the new workbook appears on the taskbar.

SWITCH BETWEEN WORKBOOKS

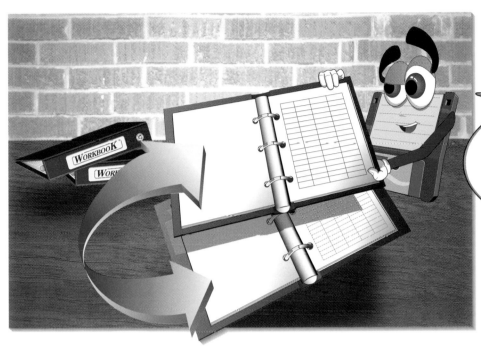

Excel lets you have many workbooks open at once. You can easily switch from one open workbook to another.

SWITCH BETWEEN WORKBOOKS

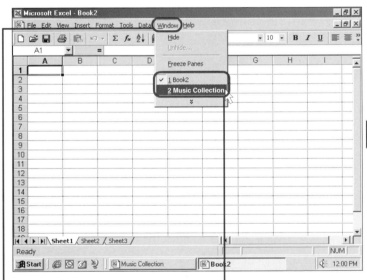

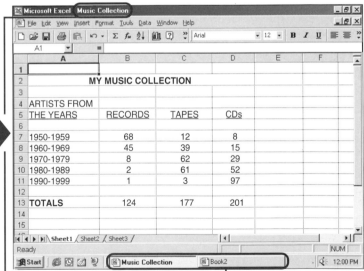

1 Click **Window** to display a list of all the workbooks you have open.

2 Click the name of the workbook you want to switch to.

■ The workbook appears.

■ Excel displays the name of the current workbook at the top of your screen.

■ The taskbar displays a button for each open workbook. You can also switch to a workbook by clicking its button on the taskbar.

When you finish using a workbook, you can close the workbook to remove it from your screen.

When you close a workbook, you do not exit the Excel program. You can continue to work with other workbooks.

CLOSE A WORKBOOK

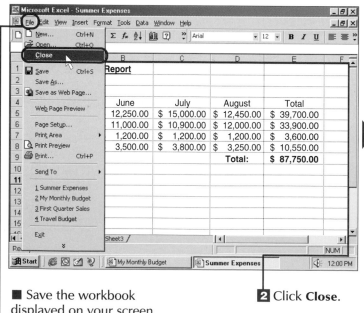

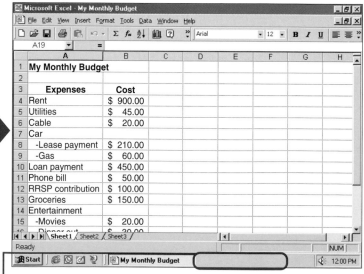

■ Save the workbook displayed on your screen before closing the workbook. To save a workbook, see page 28.

1 Click **File**.

2 Click **Close**.

■ The workbook disappears from your screen.

■ The button for the workbook disappears from the taskbar.

■ If you had more than one workbook open, the second last workbook you worked with appears on your screen.

When you finish using Excel, you can exit the program.

To prevent the loss of data, you should always exit all open programs before turning off your computer.

EXIT EXCEL

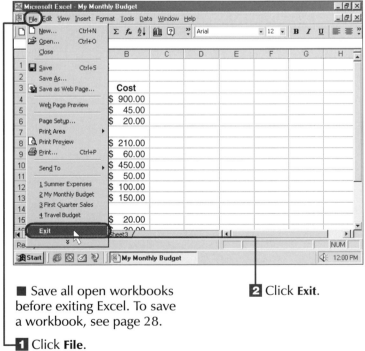

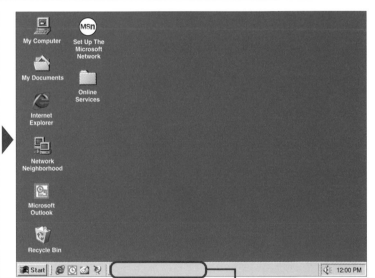

■ Save all open workbooks before exiting Excel. To save a workbook, see page 28.

1 Click **File**.

2 Click **Exit**.

■ The Microsoft Excel window disappears from your screen.

■ The button for the program disappears from the taskbar.

OPEN A WORKBOOK

You can open a saved workbook and display it on your screen. This allows you to review and make changes to the workbook.

OPEN A WORKBOOK

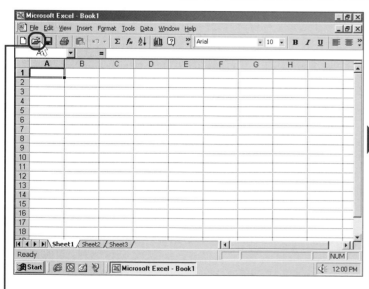

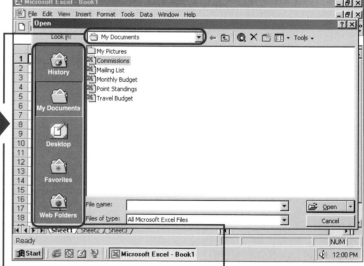

1 Click 📂 to open a workbook.

Note: If 📂 is not displayed, click ⏵ on the Standard toolbar to display all the buttons.

■ The Open dialog box appears.

■ This area shows the location of the displayed workbooks. You can click this area to change the location.

■ This area allows you to access commonly used folders. To display the contents of a folder, click the folder.

Note: For information on the commonly used folders, see the top of page 29.

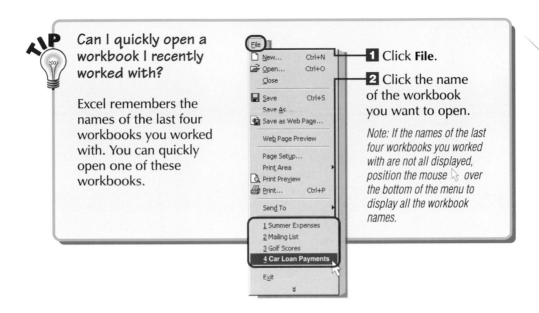

TIP

Can I quickly open a workbook I recently worked with?

Excel remembers the names of the last four workbooks you worked with. You can quickly open one of these workbooks.

1 Click **File**.

2 Click the name of the workbook you want to open.

Note: If the names of the last four workbooks you worked with are not all displayed, position the mouse over the bottom of the menu to display all the workbook names.

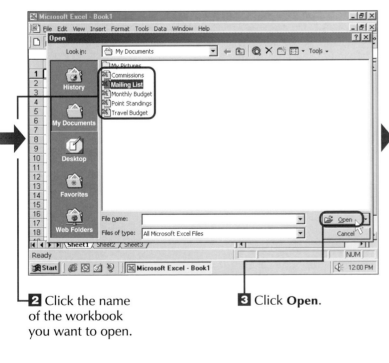

2 Click the name of the workbook you want to open.

3 Click **Open**.

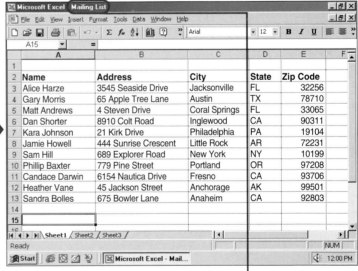

■ Excel opens the workbook and displays it on your screen. You can now review and make changes to the workbook.

■ The name of the workbook appears at the top of your screen.

FIND A WORKBOOK

If you cannot remember the name or location of a workbook you want to open, you can search for the workbook.

FIND A WORKBOOK

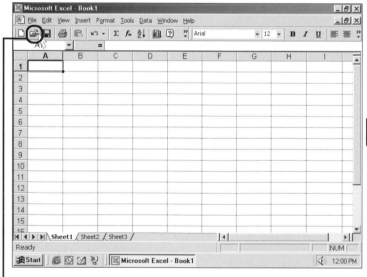

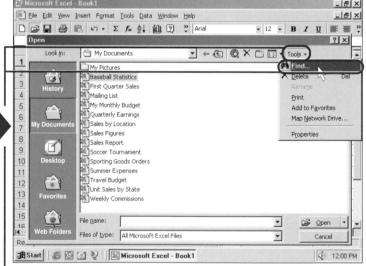

1 Click 📂 to display the Open dialog box.

Note: If 📂 is not displayed, click ⁝ on the Standard toolbar to display all the buttons.

■ The Open dialog box appears.

2 Click **Tools**.

3 Click **Find**.

■ The Find dialog box appears.

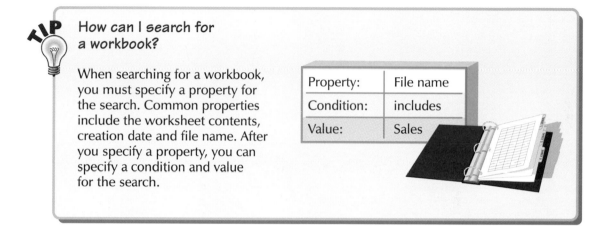

How can I search for a workbook?

When searching for a workbook, you must specify a property for the search. Common properties include the worksheet contents, creation date and file name. After you specify a property, you can specify a condition and value for the search.

Property:	File name
Condition:	includes
Value:	Sales

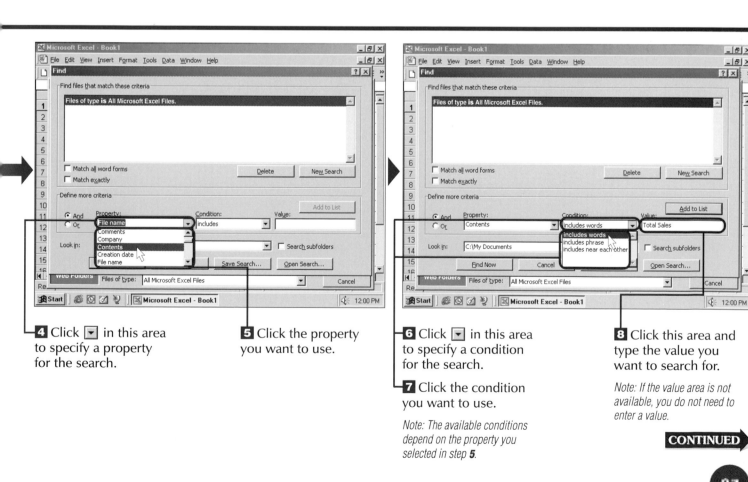

4 Click ▼ in this area to specify a property for the search.

5 Click the property you want to use.

6 Click ▼ in this area to specify a condition for the search.

7 Click the condition you want to use.

Note: The available conditions depend on the property you selected in step **5**.

8 Click this area and type the value you want to search for.

Note: If the value area is not available, you do not need to enter a value.

CONTINUED

37

FIND A WORKBOOK (CONTINUED)

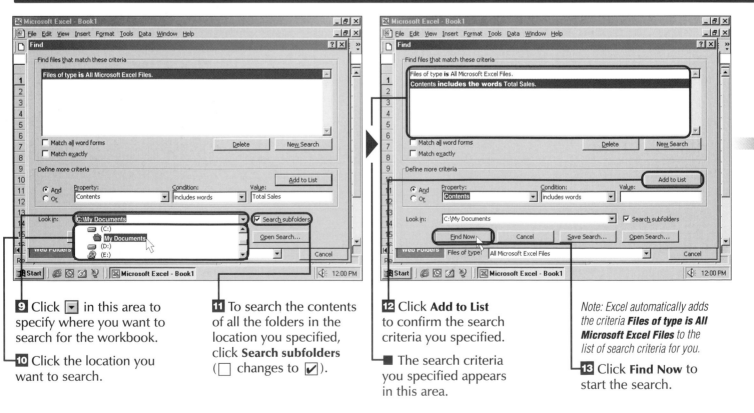

9 Click ▼ in this area to specify where you want to search for the workbook.

10 Click the location you want to search.

11 To search the contents of all the folders in the location you specified, click **Search subfolders** (☐ changes to ☑).

12 Click **Add to List** to confirm the search criteria you specified.

■ The search criteria you specified appears in this area.

*Note: Excel automatically adds the criteria **Files of type is All Microsoft Excel Files** to the list of search criteria for you.*

13 Click **Find Now** to start the search.

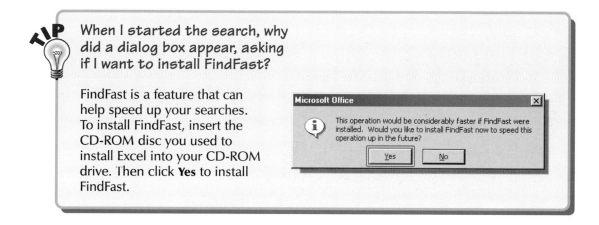

When I started the search, why did a dialog box appear, asking if I want to install FindFast?

FindFast is a feature that can help speed up your searches. To install FindFast, insert the CD-ROM disc you used to install Excel into your CD-ROM drive. Then click **Yes** to install FindFast.

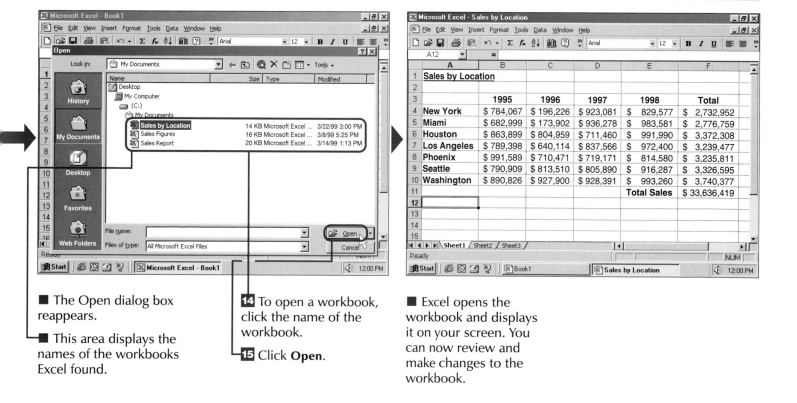

■ The Open dialog box reappears.

■ This area displays the names of the workbooks Excel found.

14 To open a workbook, click the name of the workbook.

15 Click **Open**.

■ Excel opens the workbook and displays it on your screen. You can now review and make changes to the workbook.

CHAPTER 3

EDIT YOUR WORKSHEETS

Do you want to edit the data in your worksheet or check your worksheet for spelling errors? This chapter teaches you how.

Edit Data 42

Delete Data .44

Undo Changes 45

Move or Copy Data 46

Check Spelling 50

Find Data 52

Replace Data 54

Insert a Row or Column 56

Delete a Row or Column 58

Name Cells 60

You can edit data in your worksheet to correct a mistake or update the data.

EDIT DATA

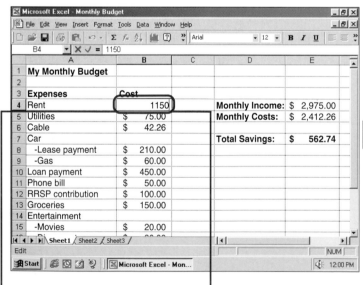

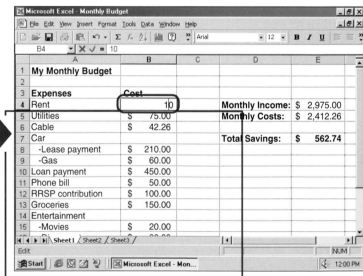

1 Double-click the cell containing the data you want to edit.

■ A flashing insertion point appears in the cell.

2 Press the ← or → key to move the insertion point to where you want to remove or insert characters.

3 To remove the character to the left of the insertion point, press the ◆Backspace key.

■ To remove the character to the right of the insertion point, press the Delete key.

42

TIP

How do I use the number keys on the right side of my keyboard to insert numbers?

When **NUM** appears at the bottom of your screen, you can use the number keys on the right side of your keyboard to insert numbers.

■ To turn the display of **NUM** on or off, press the Num Lock key.

REPLACE ALL DATA IN A CELL

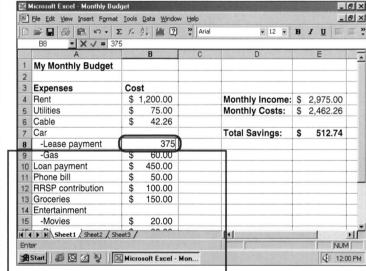

4 To insert data where the insertion point flashes on your screen, type the data.

5 When you finish making changes to the data, press the Enter key.

1 Click the cell containing the data you want to replace with new data.

2 Type the new data and then press the Enter key.

DELETE DATA

You can remove data you no longer need from cells in your worksheet.

You can delete data from a single cell or from several cells at once.

DELETE DATA

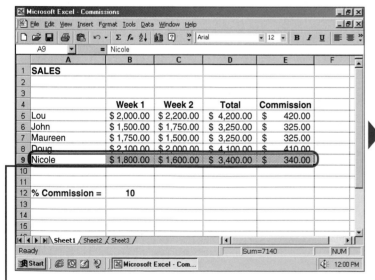

1 Select the cells containing the data you want to delete. To select cells, see page 12.

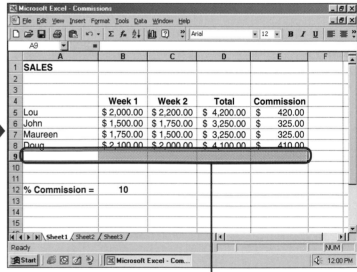

2 Press the Delete key.

■ The data in the cells you selected disappears.

UNDO CHANGES

Excel remembers the last changes you made to your worksheet. If you regret these changes, you can cancel them by using the Undo feature.

The Undo feature can cancel your last editing and formatting changes.

UNDO CHANGES

1 Click 🔄 to undo the last change you made to your worksheet.

Note: If 🔄 is not displayed, click 🔧 on the Standard toolbar to display all the buttons.

■ Excel cancels the last change you made to your worksheet.

■ You can repeat step **1** to cancel previous changes you made.

■ To reverse the results of using the Undo feature, click 🔄.

Note: If 🔄 is not displayed, click 🔧 on the Standard toolbar to display all the buttons.

45

MOVE OR COPY DATA

You can move or copy data to a new location in your worksheet by dragging and dropping the data. This method is useful when moving or copying data short distances in your worksheet.

USING DRAG AND DROP

1 Select the cells containing the data you want to move or copy. To select cells, see page 12.

2 Position the mouse ⊕ over a border of the selected cells (⊕ changes to ⬚).

What is the difference between moving and copying data?

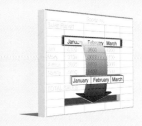

Moving data

Moving data allows you to reorganize data in your worksheet. When you move data, the data disappears from its original location in your worksheet.

Copying data

Copying data allows you to repeat data in your worksheet without having to retype the data. When you copy data, the data appears in both the original and new location.

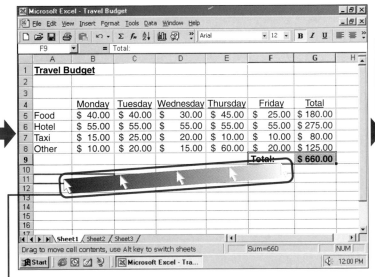

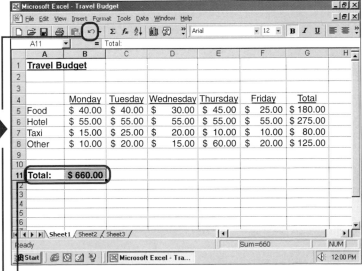

3 To move the data, drag the mouse ⬚ to where you want to place the data.

■ To copy the data, press and hold down the **Ctrl** key as you drag the mouse ⬚ to where you want to place the data.

Note: A gray box indicates where the data will appear.

■ The data appears in the new location.

■ To immediately cancel the move or copy, click 🔄.

Note: If 🔄 is not displayed, click 📋 on the Standard toolbar to display all the buttons.

MOVE OR COPY DATA

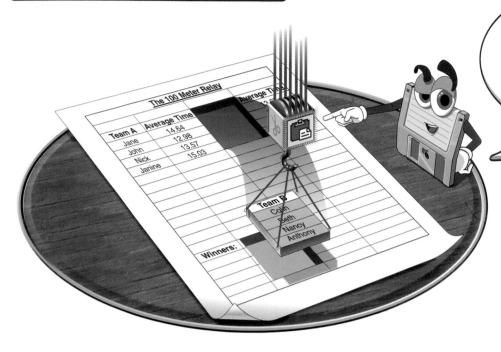

You can move or copy data to a new location in your worksheet by using toolbar buttons. This method is useful when moving or copying data long distances in your worksheet.

USING THE TOOLBAR BUTTONS

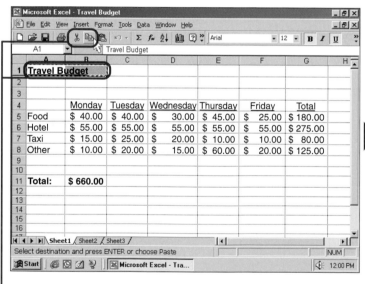

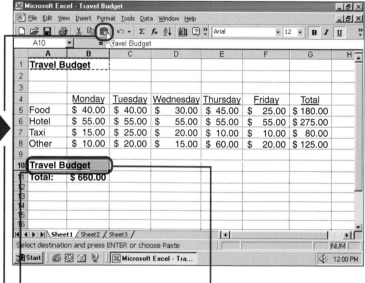

1 Select the cells containing the data you want to move or copy. To select cells, see page 12.

2 Click one of the following buttons.

✂ Move data

▣ Copy data

Note: If the button you want is not displayed, click ⟩⟩ on the Standard toolbar to display all the buttons.

3 Click the cell where you want to place the data. This cell will become the top left cell of the new location.

4 Click ▣ to place the data in the new location.

Note: If ▣ is not displayed, click ⟩⟩ on the Standard toolbar to display all the buttons.

■ The data appears in the new location.

48

Can I use the Clipboard toolbar to move or copy a formula in my worksheet?

No. When you use the Clipboard toolbar to move or copy a formula in your worksheet, Excel places only the result of the formula in the new location. If you change the data used in the original formula, the result in the new location will not change. For information on formulas, see page 64.

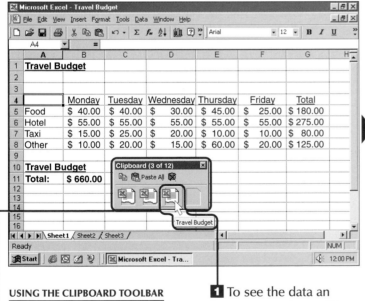

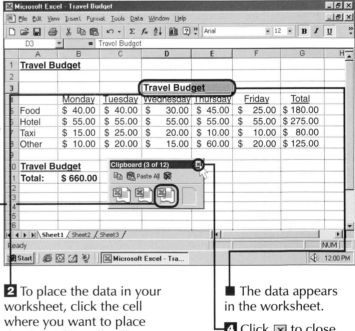

USING THE CLIPBOARD TOOLBAR

■ The Clipboard toolbar may appear when you move or copy data using the toolbar buttons. Each icon on the toolbar represents data you have selected to move or copy.

Note: To display the Clipboard toolbar, see page 21.

1 To see the data an icon represents, position the mouse ⍉ over the icon. A yellow box appears, displaying the data.

2 To place the data in your worksheet, click the cell where you want to place the data. This cell will become the top left cell of the new location.

3 Click the icon to place the data in your worksheet.

■ The data appears in the worksheet.

4 Click ☒ to close the Clipboard toolbar.

Excel compares every word in your worksheet to words in its dictionary. If a word in your worksheet does not exist in the dictionary, Excel considers the word misspelled.

CHECK SPELLING

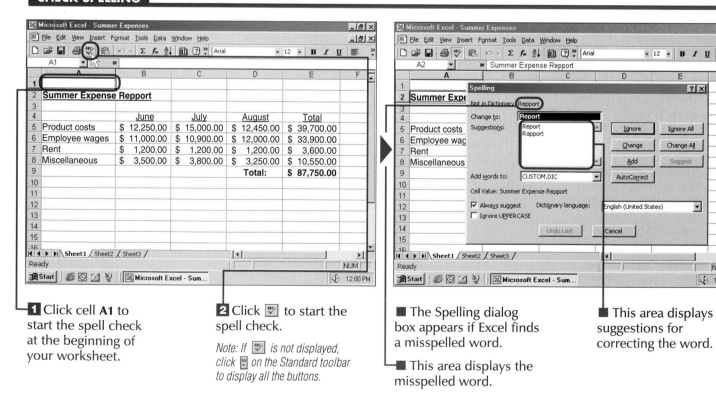

1 Click cell **A1** to start the spell check at the beginning of your worksheet.

2 Click 🅰️ to start the spell check.

Note: If 🅰️ is not displayed, click 🔽 on the Standard toolbar to display all the buttons.

■ The Spelling dialog box appears if Excel finds a misspelled word.

■ This area displays the misspelled word.

■ This area displays suggestions for correcting the word.

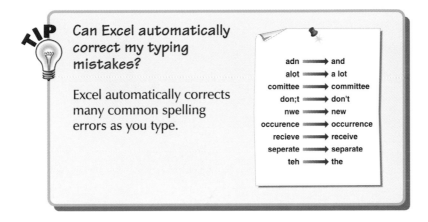

Can Excel automatically correct my typing mistakes?

Excel automatically corrects many common spelling errors as you type.

adn	➡	and
alot	➡	a lot
comittee	➡	committee
don;t	➡	don't
nwe	➡	new
occurence	➡	occurrence
recieve	➡	receive
seperate	➡	separate
teh	➡	the

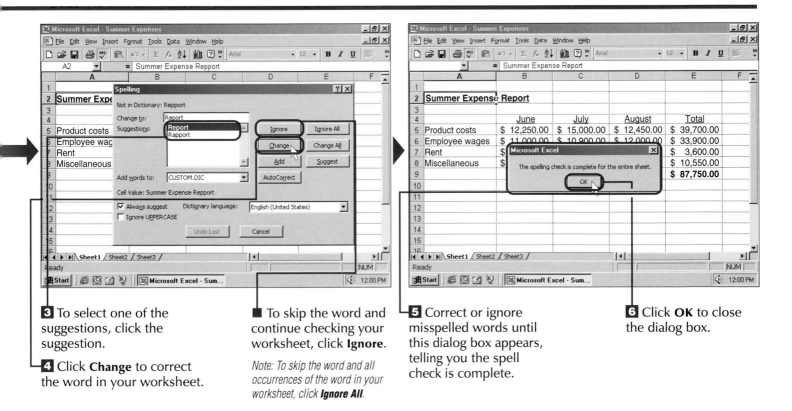

3 To select one of the suggestions, click the suggestion.

4 Click **Change** to correct the word in your worksheet.

■ To skip the word and continue checking your worksheet, click **Ignore**.

*Note: To skip the word and all occurrences of the word in your worksheet, click **Ignore All**.*

5 Correct or ignore misspelled words until this dialog box appears, telling you the spell check is complete.

6 Click **OK** to close the dialog box.

You can use the Find feature to quickly locate a word or number in your worksheet.

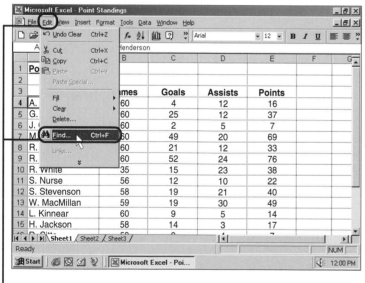

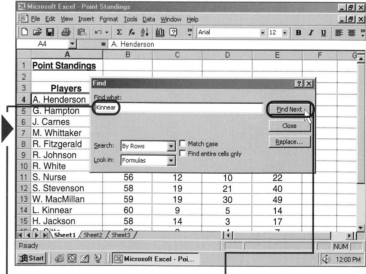

1 Click **Edit**.

2 Click **Find**.

■ The Find dialog box appears.

3 Type the word or number you want to find.

4 Click **Find Next** to start the search.

*Note: A dialog box appears if Excel cannot find the word or number you specified. Click **OK** to close the dialog box. Then skip to step **6**.*

TIP

Can I search for part of a word or number?

When you search for data in your worksheet, Excel will find the data you specify even if the data is part of a larger word or number. For example, if you search for the number **105**, Excel will also find the numbers **105.35**, **2105** and **1056**.

Find: 105

105.35 2105 1056

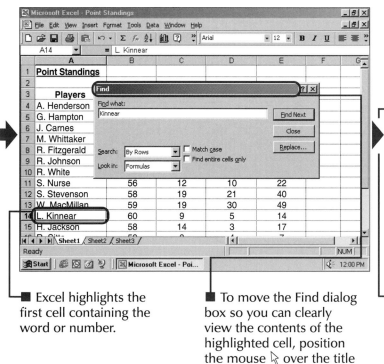

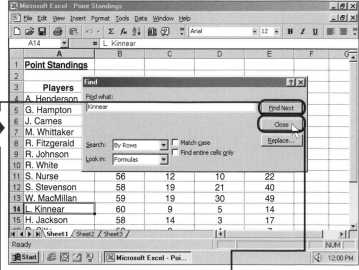

■ Excel highlights the first cell containing the word or number.

■ To move the Find dialog box so you can clearly view the contents of the highlighted cell, position the mouse ⃗ over the title bar and then drag the dialog box to a new location.

5 Click **Find Next** to find the next matching word or number. Repeat this step until you find the word or number you are searching for.

6 To close the Find dialog box at any time, click **Close**.

The Replace feature can locate and replace every occurrence of a word or number in your worksheet. This is useful if you have incorrectly entered data throughout your worksheet.

REPLACE DATA

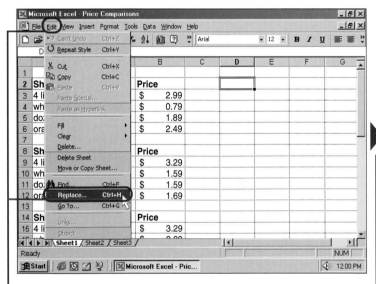

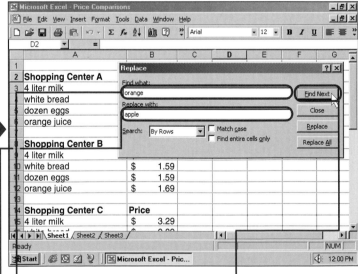

1 Click **Edit**.

2 Click **Replace**.

Note: If Replace does not appear on the menu, position the mouse � over the bottom of the menu to display all the menu commands.

■ The Replace dialog box appears.

3 Type the word or number you want to replace with new data.

4 Press the Tab key and then type the new word or number.

5 Click **Find Next** to start the search.

54

**Can Excel find and replace a
number used in my formulas?**

Excel automatically searches the
formulas in your worksheet for the
number you specified. This is useful if
you want to change a number used in
several formulas. For example, if sales
tax increases from 7% to 8%, you can
search for all occurrences of **.07** in your
formulas and replace them with **.08**.

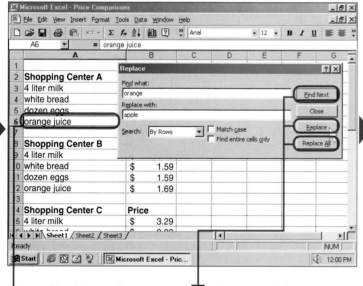

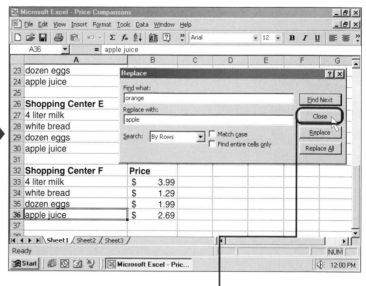

■ Excel highlights the
first cell containing the
word or number you
specified.

6 Click one of the
following options.

Find Next - Ignore word
or number

Replace - Replace word
or number

Replace All - Replace all
occurrences of word or
number in the worksheet

7 Repeat step **6** until you
find all the occurrences
of the word or number
you want to replace.

8 Click **Close** to close
the Replace dialog box.

INSERT A ROW OR COLUMN

You can add a row or column to your worksheet when you want to insert additional data.

INSERT A ROW

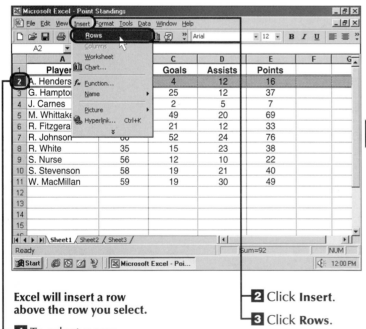

Excel will insert a row above the row you select.

1 To select a row, click the row number.

2 Click **Insert**.

3 Click **Rows**.

■ The new row appears and all the rows that follow shift downward.

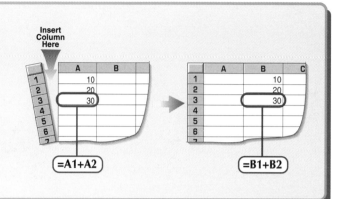

TIP

Do I need to adjust my
formulas when I insert
a row or column?

When you insert a row
or column, Excel
automatically updates
any formulas affected
by the insertion. For
information on formulas,
see page 64.

INSERT A COLUMN

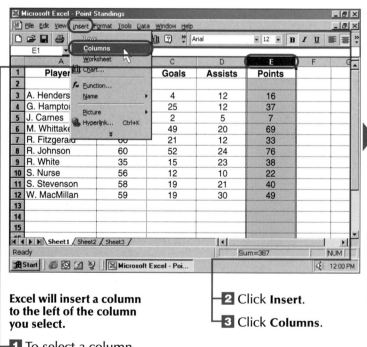

**Excel will insert a column
to the left of the column
you select.**

1 To select a column,
click the column letter.

2 Click **Insert**.

3 Click **Columns**.

■ The new column appears
and all the columns that
follow shift to the right.

DELETE A ROW OR COLUMN

You can delete a row or column from your worksheet to remove cells and data you no longer need.

DELETE A ROW

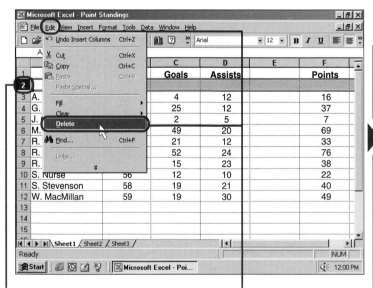

1 To select the row you want to delete, click the row number.

2 Click **Edit**.

3 Click **Delete** to delete the row.

■ The row disappears and all the rows that follow shift upward.

■ To immediately return the row to the worksheet, click 🔄.

Note: If 🔄 is not displayed, click ⏵ on the Standard toolbar to display all the buttons.

Why did #REF! appear
in a cell after I deleted
a row or column?

If **#REF!** appears in a cell in
your worksheet, you deleted
data needed to calculate a
formula. Before you delete a
row or column, make sure the
row or column does not contain
data that is used in a formula.
For information on formulas,
see page 64.

DELETE A COLUMN

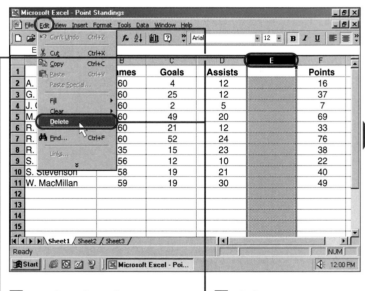

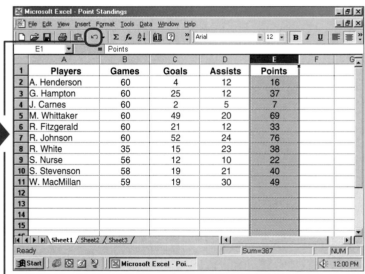

1 To select the column
you want to delete,
click the column letter.

2 Click **Edit**.

3 Click **Delete** to
delete the column.

■ The column disappears
and all the columns that
follow shift to the left.

■ To immediately return
the column to the
worksheet, click 🔄.

*Note: If 🔄 is not displayed,
click ❯ on the Standard toolbar
to display all the buttons.*

You can give cells in your worksheet a meaningful name. Using named cells can save you time when selecting cells or entering formulas.

You can name a single cell or a range of cells in your worksheet.

NAME CELLS

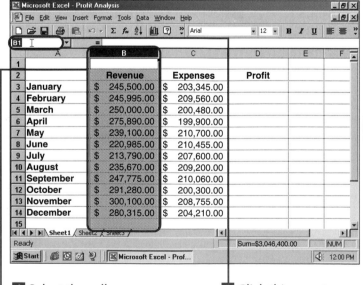

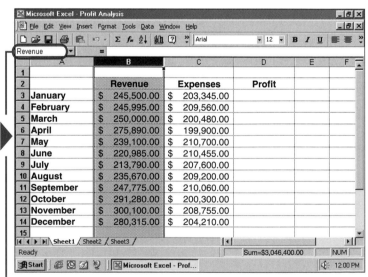

1 Select the cells you want to name. To select cells, see page 12.

2 Click this area to highlight the existing information.

3 Type the name you want to use for the cells. The name cannot start with a number or contain spaces.

4 Press the Enter key to name the cells.

60

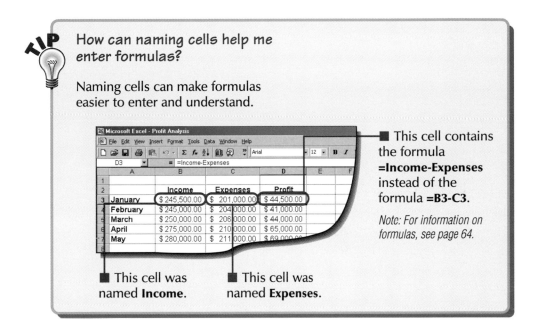

TIP

How can naming cells help me enter formulas?

Naming cells can make formulas easier to enter and understand.

■ This cell contains the formula **=Income-Expenses** instead of the formula **=B3-C3**.

Note: For information on formulas, see page 64.

■ This cell was named **Income**.

■ This cell was named **Expenses**.

SELECT NAMED CELLS

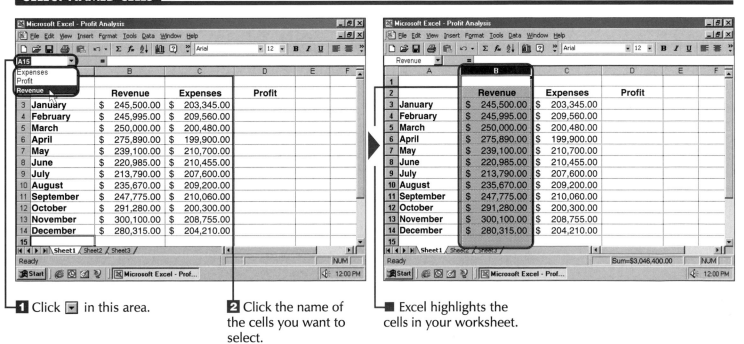

1 Click ▼ in this area.

2 Click the name of the cells you want to select.

■ Excel highlights the cells in your worksheet.

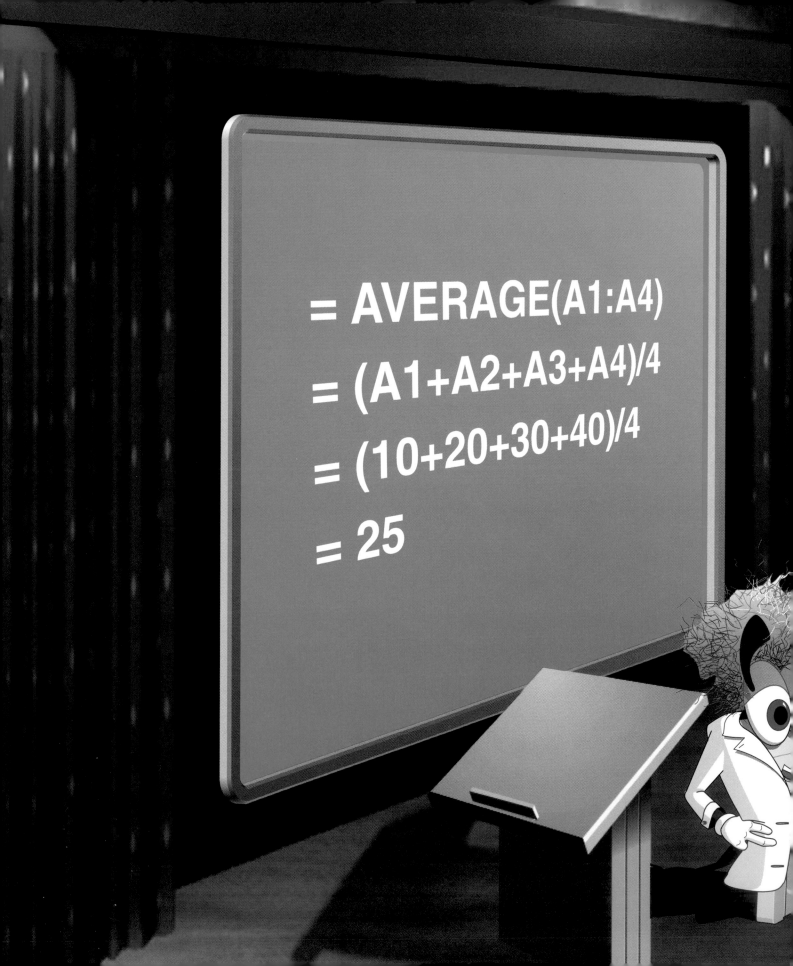

CHAPTER 4

WORK WITH FORMULAS AND FUNCTIONS

Would you like to perform calculations on the data in your worksheet? Learn how in this chapter.

Introduction to Formulas 64

Enter a Formula 66

Introduction to Functions 68

Enter a Function 70

Using AutoCalculate 74

Add Numbers .76

Copy a Formula 78

Errors in Formulas 82

A formula allows you to calculate and analyze data in your worksheet.

A1+A2+A3

A formula always begins with an equal sign (=).

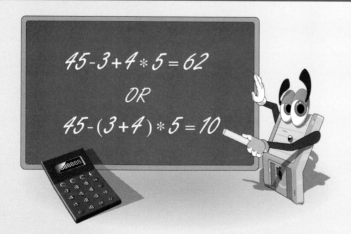

$45-3+4*5=62$

OR

$45-(3+4)*5=10$

Order of Calculations

Excel performs calculations in the following order:

1 Exponents (^)

2 Multiplication (*) and Division (/)

3 Addition (+) and Subtraction (-)

You can use parentheses ( ) to change the order in which Excel performs calculations. Excel will perform the calculations inside the parentheses first.

Cell References

When entering formulas, use cell references instead of actual data whenever possible. For example, enter the formula **=A1+A2** instead of **=10+30**.

When you use cell references and you change a number used in a formula, Excel will automatically redo the calculation for you.

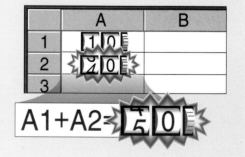

EXAMPLES OF FORMULAS

	A	B
1	10	
2	20	
3	30	
4	40	
5		
6	1230	

■ This cell contains the formula:

=A1+A2+A3*A4

=10+20+30*40

=1230

	A	B
1	10	
2	20	
3	30	
4	40	
5		
6	2010	

■ This cell contains the formula:

=A1+(A2+A3)*A4

=10+(20+30)*40

=2010

	A	B
1	10	
2	20	
3	30	
4	40	
5		
6	320	

■ This cell contains the formula:

=A1*A3-A2+A4

=10*30-20+40

=320

	A	B
1	10	
2	20	
3	30	
4	40	
5		
6	140	

■ This cell contains the formula:

=A1*(A3-A2)+A4

=10*(30-20)+40

=140

	A	B
1	10	
2	20	
3	30	
4	40	
5		
6	63	

■ This cell contains the formula:

=A3/A1+A2+A4

=30/10+20+40

=63

	A	B
1	10	
2	20	
3	30	
4	40	
5		
6	41	

■ This cell contains the formula:

=A3/(A1+A2)+A4

=30/(10+20)+40

=41

You can enter a formula into any cell in your worksheet. A formula helps you calculate and analyze data in your worksheet.

ENTER A FORMULA

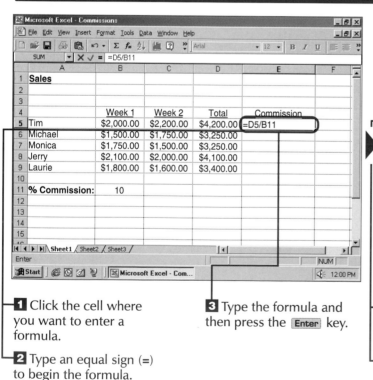

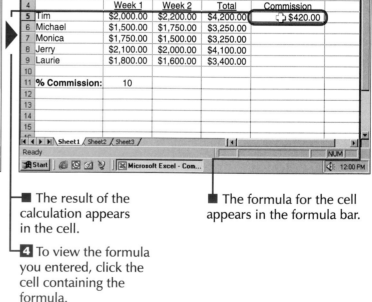

1 Click the cell where you want to enter a formula.

2 Type an equal sign (=) to begin the formula.

3 Type the formula and then press the **Enter** key.

■ The result of the calculation appears in the cell.

4 To view the formula you entered, click the cell containing the formula.

■ The formula for the cell appears in the formula bar.

**What happens if I change a
number used in a formula?**

If you change a number
used in a formula, Excel
will automatically redo
the calculation for you.

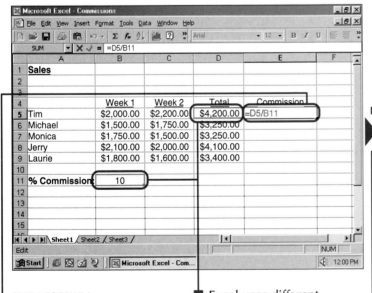

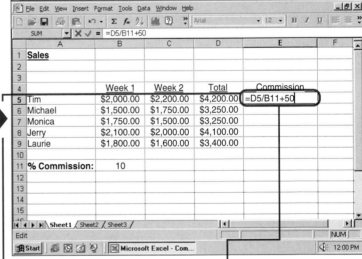

EDIT A FORMULA

1 Double-click the cell
containing the formula
you want to change.

■ The formula appears
in the cell.

■ Excel uses different
colors to outline each
cell used in the formula.

2 Press the ← or →
key to move the flashing
insertion point to where
you want to remove or
add characters.

3 To remove the
character to the left
of the insertion point,
press the +Backspace key.

4 To add data where
the insertion point
flashes on your
screen, type the data.

5 When you finish
making changes to
the formula, press
the Enter key.

A function is a ready-to-use formula that you can use to perform a calculation on the data in your worksheet.

INTRODUCTION TO FUNCTIONS

■ A function always begins with an equal sign (=).

■ The data Excel will use to calculate a function is enclosed in parentheses ( ).

```
=SUM(A1,A2,A3)

=AVERAGE(C1,C2,C3)

=MAX(B7,C7,D7,E7)

=COUNT(D12,D13,D14)
```

```
=SUM(A1:A3)

=AVERAGE(C1:C3)

=MAX(B7:E7)

=COUNT(D12:D14)
```

Specify Individual Cells

When a comma (,) separates cell references in a function, Excel uses each cell to perform the calculation.

For example, =SUM(A1,A2,A3) is the same as the formula =A1+A2+A3.

Specify Group of Cells

When a colon (:) separates cell references in a function, Excel uses the specified cells and all cells between them to perform the calculation.

For example, =SUM(A1:A3) is the same as the formula =A1+A2+A3.

COMMON FUNCTIONS

Average

Calculates the average value of a list of numbers.

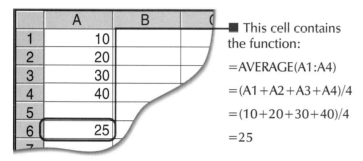

■ This cell contains the function:

=AVERAGE(A1:A4)

=(A1+A2+A3+A4)/4

=(10+20+30+40)/4

=25

Count

Calculates the number of values in a list.

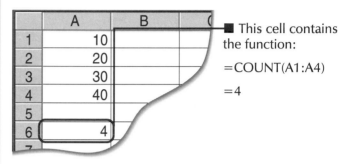

■ This cell contains the function:

=COUNT(A1:A4)

=4

Max

Finds the largest value in a list of numbers.

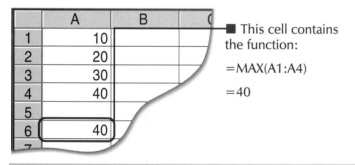

■ This cell contains the function:

=MAX(A1:A4)

=40

Min

Finds the smallest value in a list of numbers.

■ This cell contains the function:

=MIN(A1:A4)

=10

Sum

Adds a list of numbers.

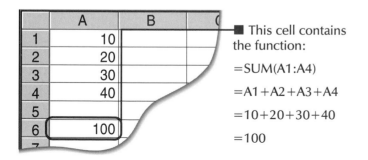

■ This cell contains the function:

=SUM(A1:A4)

=A1+A2+A3+A4

=10+20+30+40

=100

Round

Rounds a value to a specific number of digits.

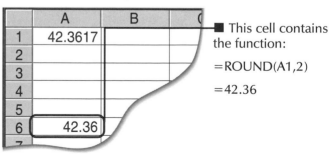

■ This cell contains the function:

=ROUND(A1,2)

=42.36

ENTER A FUNCTION

Excel helps you enter functions in your worksheet. Functions let you perform calculations without typing long, complex formulas.

=SUM(A1:A4)

=AVERAGE(A1:A4)

=ROUND(E4,2)

=COUNT(B1:B6)

=MAX(E1:E4)

ENTER A FUNCTION

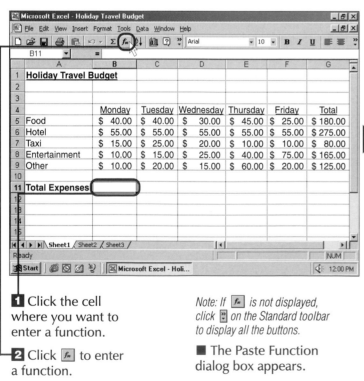

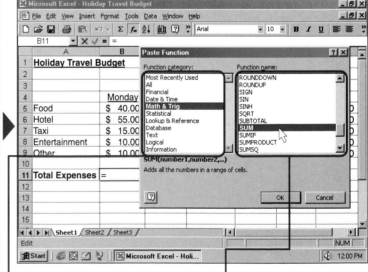

1 Click the cell where you want to enter a function.

2 Click ƒₓ to enter a function.

Note: If ƒₓ is not displayed, click » on the Standard toolbar to display all the buttons.

■ The Paste Function dialog box appears.

3 Click the category containing the function you want to use.

*Note: If you do not know which category contains the function you want to use, select **All** to display a list of all the functions.*

■ This area displays the functions in the category you selected.

4 Click the function you want to use.

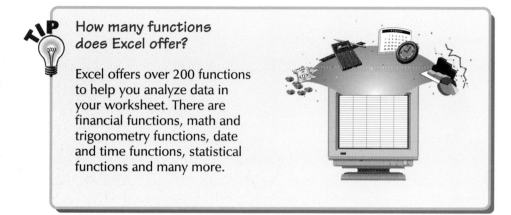

TIP

How many functions does Excel offer?

Excel offers over 200 functions to help you analyze data in your worksheet. There are financial functions, math and trigonometry functions, date and time functions, statistical functions and many more.

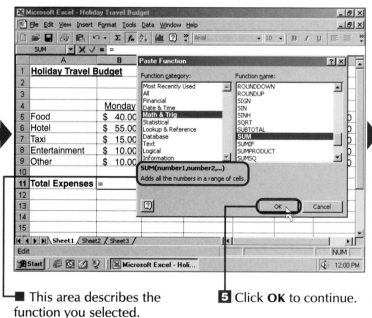

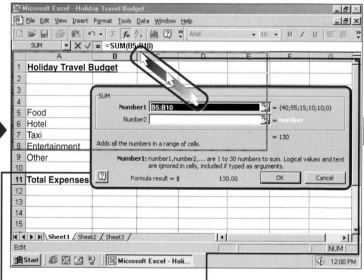

■ This area describes the function you selected.

5 Click **OK** to continue.

■ A dialog box appears. If the dialog box covers data you want to use in the calculation, you can move the dialog box to a new location.

6 To move the dialog box, position the mouse ⌖ over a blank area in the dialog box and then drag the dialog box to a new location.

CONTINUED

When entering a function, you must specify which numbers you want to use in the calculation.

=SUM(D1:D4)

	A	B	C	D
1	100	12	128	20
2	200	22	601	60
3	400	68	288	80
4	800	21	204	97

ENTER A FUNCTION (CONTINUED)

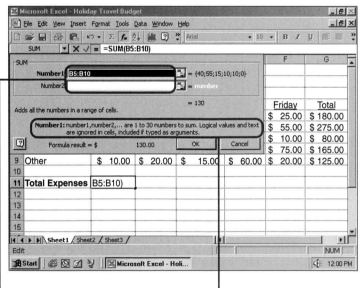

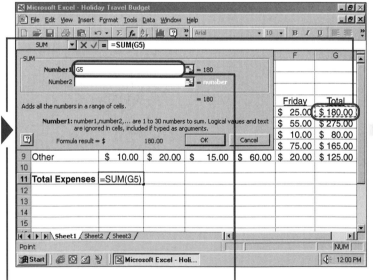

■ This area displays boxes where you enter the numbers you want to use in the calculation.

■ This area describes the numbers you need to enter.

7 To enter a number for the function, click the cell that contains the number.

Note: If the number you want to use does not appear in your worksheet, type the number.

■ The cell reference for the number appears in this area.

72

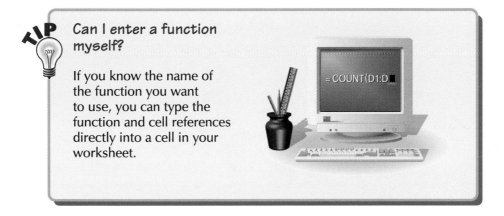

Can I enter a function myself?

If you know the name of the function you want to use, you can type the function and cell references directly into a cell in your worksheet.

=COUNT(D1:D█

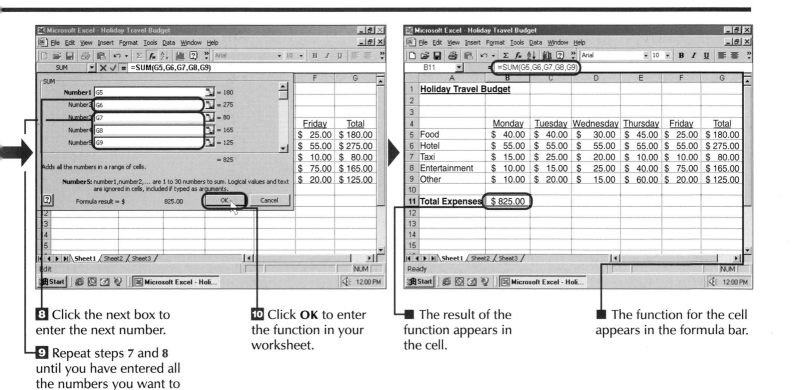

8 Click the next box to enter the next number.

9 Repeat steps **7** and **8** until you have entered all the numbers you want to use in the calculation.

10 Click **OK** to enter the function in your worksheet.

■ The result of the function appears in the cell.

■ The function for the cell appears in the formula bar.

USING AUTOCALCULATE

You can view the results of common calculations without entering a formula into your worksheet.

USING AUTOCALCULATE

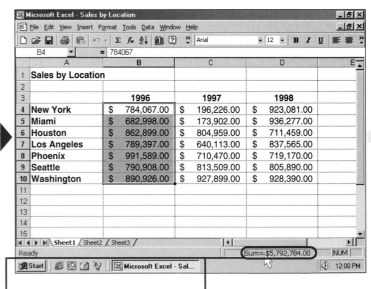

1 Select the cells you want to include in the calculation. To select cells, see page 12.

■ This area displays the sum of the cells you selected.

2 To display the result for a different calculation, right-click this area.

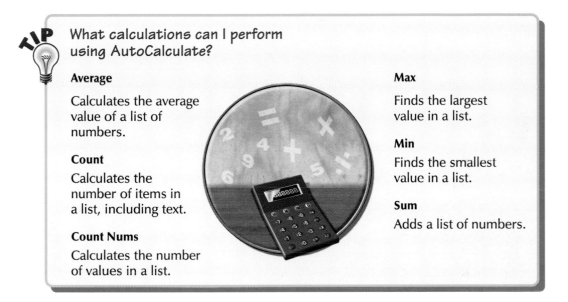

TIP

What calculations can I perform using AutoCalculate?

Average

Calculates the average value of a list of numbers.

Count

Calculates the number of items in a list, including text.

Count Nums

Calculates the number of values in a list.

Max

Finds the largest value in a list.

Min

Finds the smallest value in a list.

Sum

Adds a list of numbers.

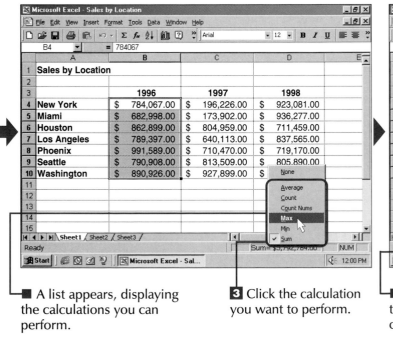

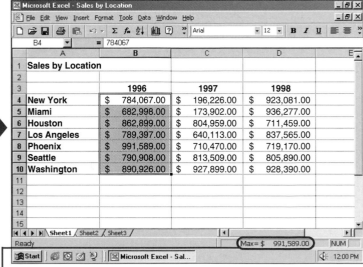

■ A list appears, displaying the calculations you can perform.

3 Click the calculation you want to perform.

■ This area displays the result for the new calculation.

You can calculate the sum of a list of numbers in your worksheet.

ADD NUMBERS

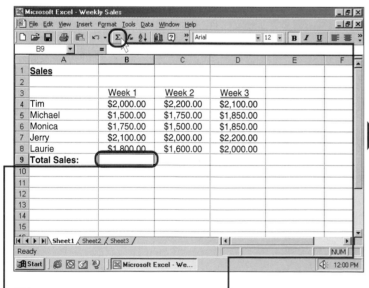

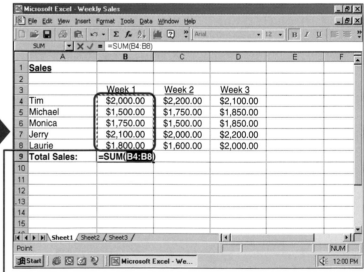

1 Click the cell below or to the right of the cells containing the numbers you want to add.

2 Click Σ to add the numbers.

Note: If Σ is not displayed, click » on the Standard toolbar to display all the buttons.

■ Excel outlines the cells it will use in the calculation with a dotted line.

■ If Excel does not outline the correct cells, select the cells containing the numbers you want to add. To select cells, see page 12.

How do I calculate the sum of rows and columns of data at the same time?

1 Select the cells containing the numbers you want to add and a blank row and column for the results. To select cells, see page 12.

2 Click Σ to perform the calculations.

	Product A	Product B	Month Totals
January	10	5	
February	20	6	
Product Totals			

	Product A	Product B	Month Totals
January	10	5	15
February	20	6	26
Product Totals	30	11	41

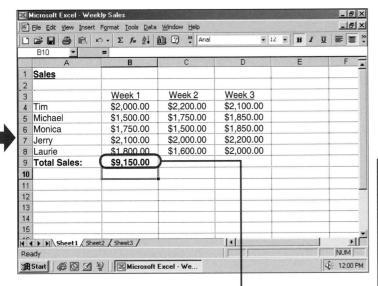

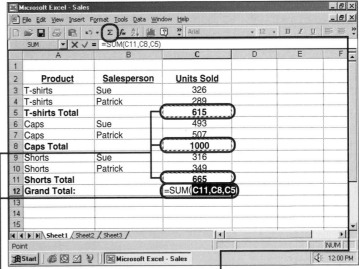

3 Press the Enter key to perform the calculation.

■ The result of the calculation appears.

CALCULATE A GRAND TOTAL

If your worksheet contains several subtotals, you can calculate a grand total.

■ These cells contain subtotals.

1 Click the cell below or to the right of the cells containing the subtotals.

2 Click Σ.

Note: If Σ is not displayed, click ░ on the Standard toolbar to display all the buttons.

3 Press the Enter key to perform the calculation.

COPY A FORMULA

If you want to use the same formula several times in your worksheet, you can save time by copying the formula.

=B2+B3+B4   =C2+C3+C4   =D2+D3+D4

COPY A FORMULA—USING RELATIVE REFERENCES

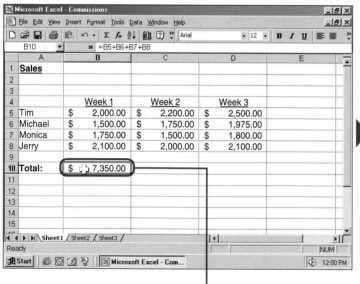

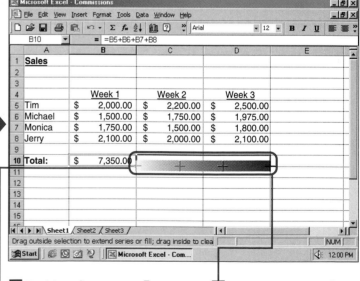

1 Enter the formula you want to copy to other cells. To enter a formula, see page 66.

*Note: In this example, cell **B10** contains the formula =B5+B6+B7+B8.*

2 Click the cell containing the formula you want to copy.

3 Position the mouse ⇩ over the bottom right corner of the cell (⇩ changes to +).

4 Drag the mouse + over the cells you want to receive a copy of the formula.

78

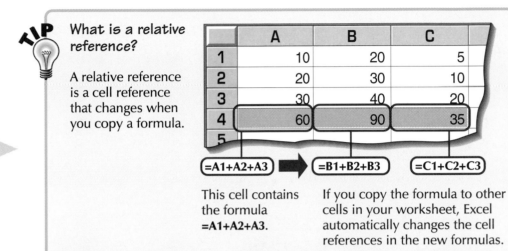

TIP

What is a relative reference?

A relative reference is a cell reference that changes when you copy a formula.

	A	B	C
1	10	20	5
2	20	30	10
3	30	40	20
4	60	90	35
5			

=A1+A2+A3 ➡ =B1+B2+B3   =C1+C2+C3

This cell contains the formula =A1+A2+A3.

If you copy the formula to other cells in your worksheet, Excel automatically changes the cell references in the new formulas.

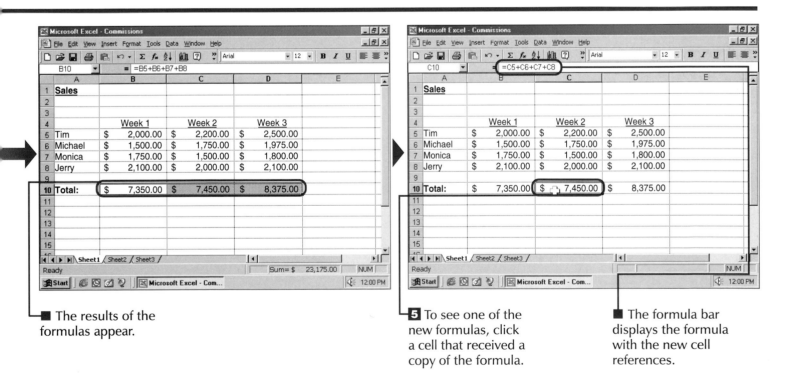

■ The results of the formulas appear.

5 To see one of the new formulas, click a cell that received a copy of the formula.

■ The formula bar displays the formula with the new cell references.

COPY A FORMULA

> You can copy a formula to other cells in your worksheet to save time. If you do not want Excel to change a cell reference when you copy a formula, you can use an absolute reference.

COPY A FORMULA–USING ABSOLUTE REFERENCES

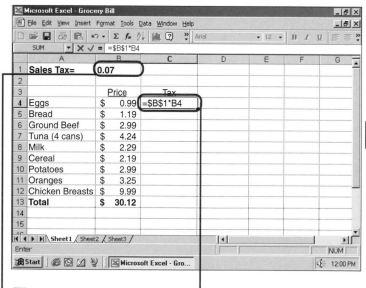

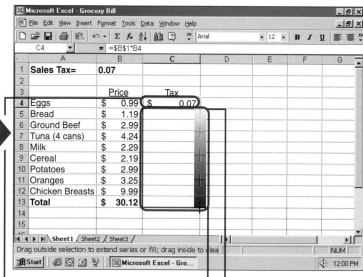

1 Enter the data you want to use in all the formulas.

2 Enter the formula you want to copy to other cells. To enter a formula, see page 66.

*Note: In this example, cell **C4** contains the formula = **$B$1*B4**.*

3 Click the cell containing the formula you want to copy.

4 Position the mouse ⊕ over the bottom right corner of the cell (⊕ changes to +).

5 Drag the mouse + over the cells you want to receive a copy of the formula.

What is an absolute reference?

An absolute reference is a cell reference that does not change when you copy a formula. To make a cell reference absolute, type a dollar sign (**$**) before both the column letter and row number, such as **$A$7**.

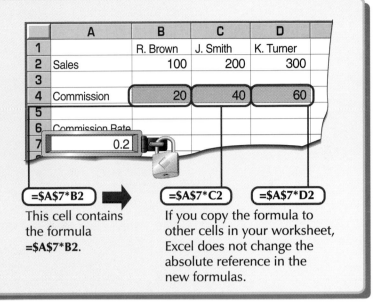

	A	B	C	D
1		R. Brown	J. Smith	K. Turner
2	Sales	100	200	300
3				
4	Commission	20	40	60
5				
6	Commission Rate			
7		0.2		

=$A$7*B2

This cell contains the formula =$A$7*B2.

=$A$7*C2   =$A$7*D2

If you copy the formula to other cells in your worksheet, Excel does not change the absolute reference in the new formulas.

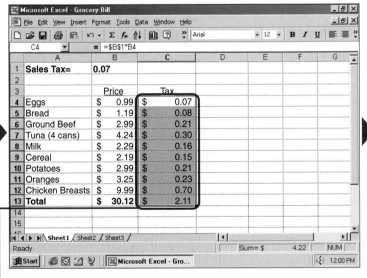

■ The results of the formulas appear.

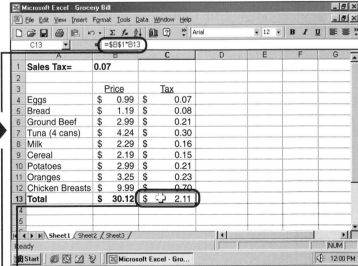

6 To see one of the new formulas, click a cell that received a copy of the formula.

■ The formula bar displays the formula with the new cell references.

■ The absolute reference (**$B$1**) in the formula did not change. The relative reference (**B13**) in the formula did change.

ERRORS IN FORMULAS

An error message appears when Excel cannot properly calculate or display the result of a formula.

Errors in formulas are often the result of typing mistakes. You can correct an error by editing the formula. To edit a formula, see page 67.

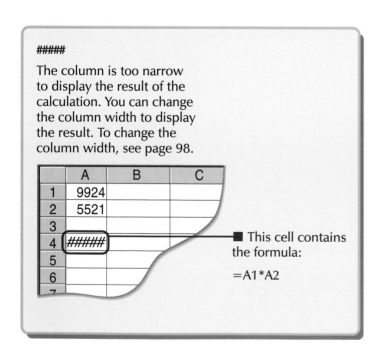

#####

The column is too narrow to display the result of the calculation. You can change the column width to display the result. To change the column width, see page 98.

■ This cell contains the formula:

=A1*A2

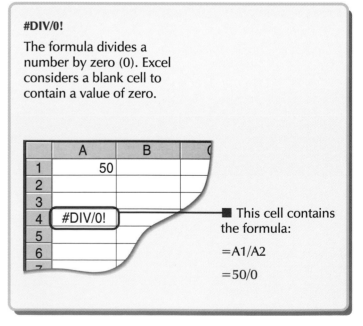

#DIV/0!

The formula divides a number by zero (0). Excel considers a blank cell to contain a value of zero.

■ This cell contains the formula:

=A1/A2

=50/0

#NAME?

The formula contains a function name or cell reference Excel does not recognize.

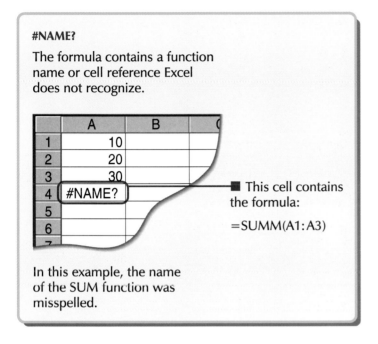

■ This cell contains the formula:

=SUMM(A1:A3)

In this example, the name of the SUM function was misspelled.

#REF!

The formula refers to a cell that is not valid.

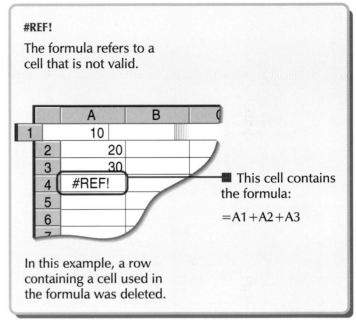

■ This cell contains the formula:

=A1+A2+A3

In this example, a row containing a cell used in the formula was deleted.

#VALUE!

The formula refers to a cell that Excel cannot use in a calculation.

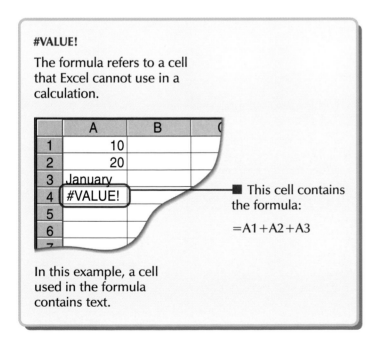

■ This cell contains the formula:

=A1+A2+A3

In this example, a cell used in the formula contains text.

Circular Reference

A warning message appears when a formula refers to the cell containing the formula. This is called a circular reference.

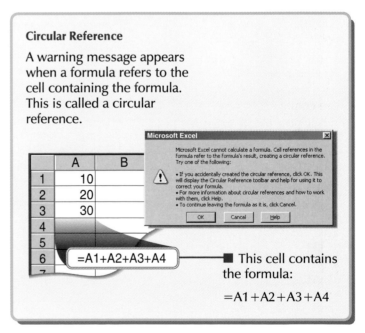

■ This cell contains the formula:

=A1+A2+A3+A4

Central Division Standings

Pool A	Games	Goals	Wins	Losses	T
Walt's Winners	6	15	4	1	
The Chargers	6	13	3	2	
Terry's Tigers	6	12	3	3	
The Breakaways	6	10	1	3	
The GO Team	6	9	1	4	
Pool B	Games		Wins	Losses	T
Brian's Boys			4	1	
The Good Guys				1	
Greg 'n' Gang	6	15		2	
The Professionals				3	
All The Way	6	13		3	
Team Spirit			1	5	

CHAPTER 5

CHANGE YOUR SCREEN DISPLAY

Are you interested in changing the way your worksheet appears on your screen? In this chapter you will learn how to zoom in and out, hide columns and more.

Display Full Screen 86

Zoom In or Out 87

Hide Columns 88

Hide Rows 90

Freeze Rows and Columns 92

Split a Worksheet 94

DISPLAY FULL SCREEN

You can display a larger working area by hiding parts of the Excel screen.

Using the full screen to view a worksheet is useful if you want to display as many cells as possible while you review and edit a large worksheet.

DISPLAY FULL SCREEN

1 Click **View**.

2 Click **Full Screen**.

Note: If Full Screen does not appear on the menu, position the mouse over the bottom of the menu to display all the menu commands.

■ Excel hides parts of the screen to display a larger working area.

■ To once again display the hidden parts of the screen, click **Close Full Screen**.

Note: You can also repeat steps 1 and 2 to once again display the hidden parts of the screen.

ZOOM IN OR OUT

Excel allows you to enlarge or reduce the display of data on your screen.

Changing the zoom setting will not affect the way data appears on a printed page.

ZOOM IN OR OUT

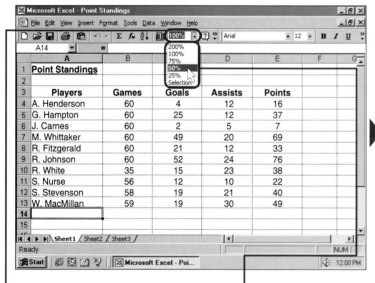

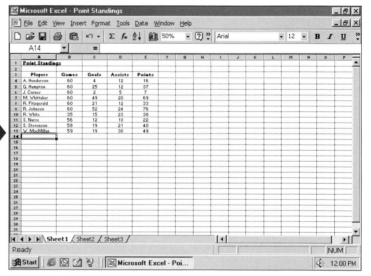

1 Click ▾ in this area to display a list of zoom settings.

Note: If the Zoom area is not displayed, click ⁑ on the Standard toolbar to display all the buttons.

2 Click the zoom setting you want to use.

■ The worksheet appears in the new zoom setting. You can edit the worksheet as usual.

■ To return to the normal zoom setting, repeat steps **1** and **2**, except select **100%** in step **2**.

HIDE COLUMNS

You can hide columns in your worksheet to reduce the amount of data displayed on your screen or hide confidential data.

You can hide a single column or multiple columns in your worksheet.

HIDE COLUMNS

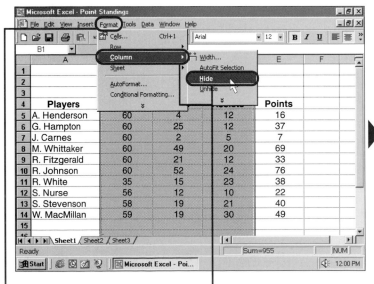

1 Select the columns you want to hide. To select columns, see page 13.

2 Click **Format**.

3 Click **Column**.

4 Click **Hide** to hide the columns.

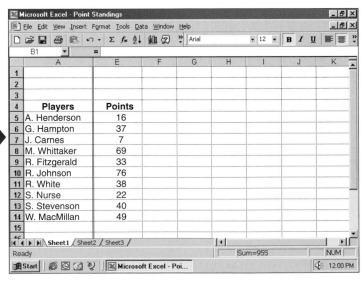

■ The columns you selected disappear from your worksheet.

Do hidden columns appear on a printed page?

Hidden columns will not appear when you print your worksheet. This is useful when you do not want to print columns that contain unneeded or confidential data.

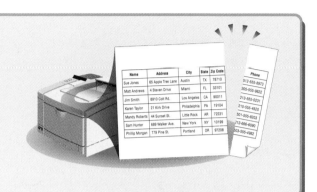

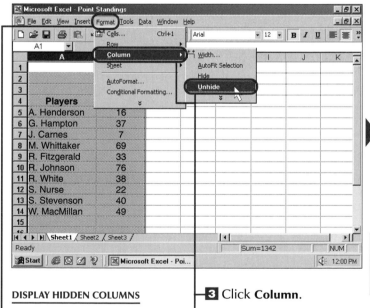

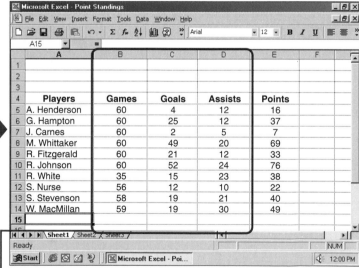

DISPLAY HIDDEN COLUMNS

1 Select the columns on each side of the hidden columns. To select columns, see page 13.

2 Click **Format**.

3 Click **Column**.

4 Click **Unhide** to display the hidden columns.

■ The hidden columns reappear in your worksheet.

■ To deselect cells, click any cell.

HIDE ROWS

You can hide rows in your worksheet to temporarily remove unnecessary or confidential data from your screen.

You can hide a single row or multiple rows in your worksheet.

HIDE ROWS

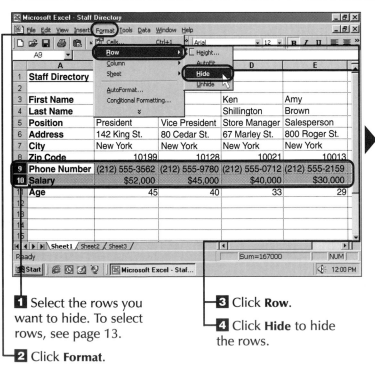

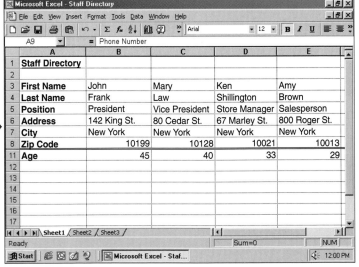

1 Select the rows you want to hide. To select rows, see page 13.

2 Click **Format**.

3 Click **Row**.

4 Click **Hide** to hide the rows.

■ The rows you selected disappear from your worksheet.

90

**Will hiding rows affect the
formulas and functions in
my worksheet?**

Hiding rows will not affect the
results of formulas and functions
in your worksheet. Excel will
use data in the hidden rows to
perform calculations even though
the data is hidden from view.
For information on formulas and
functions, see pages 64 and 68.

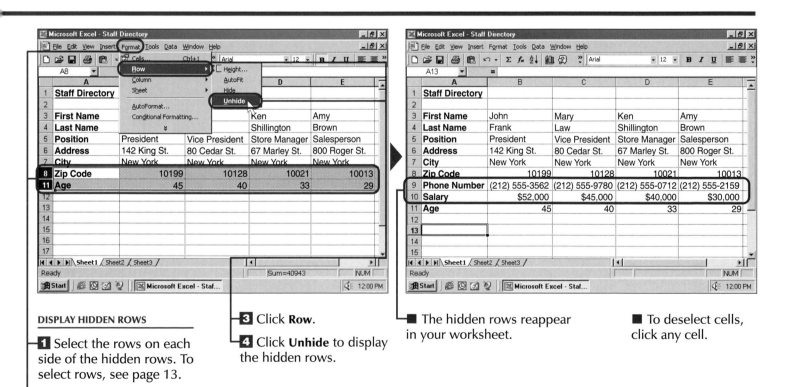

DISPLAY HIDDEN ROWS

1 Select the rows on each
side of the hidden rows. To
select rows, see page 13.

2 Click **Format**.

3 Click **Row**.

4 Click **Unhide** to display
the hidden rows.

■ The hidden rows reappear
in your worksheet.

■ To deselect cells,
click any cell.

FREEZE ROWS AND COLUMNS

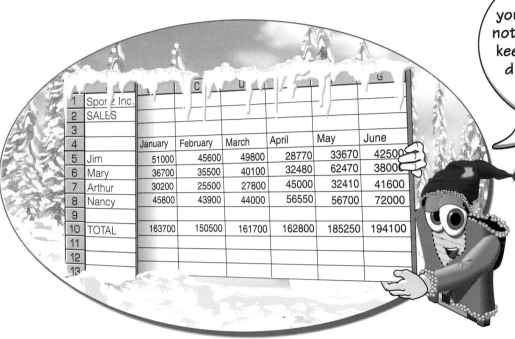

You can freeze rows and columns in your worksheet so they will not move. This allows you to keep row and column labels displayed on your screen as you move through a large worksheet.

FREEZE ROWS AND COLUMNS

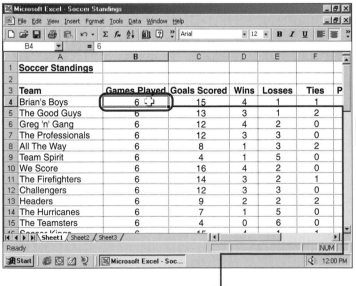

Excel will freeze the rows above and the columns to the left of the cell you select.

1 To select a cell, click the cell.

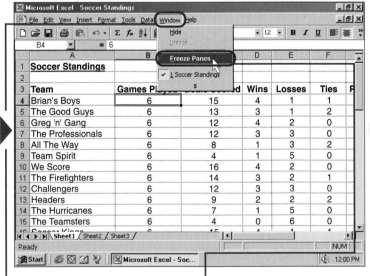

2 Click **Window**.

3 Click **Freeze Panes**.

92

How do I unfreeze rows and columns in my worksheet?

When you no longer want to keep rows and columns frozen on your screen, perform steps **2** and **3** below, except select **Unfreeze Panes** in step **3**.

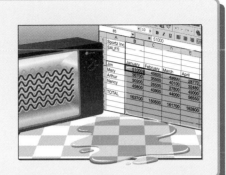

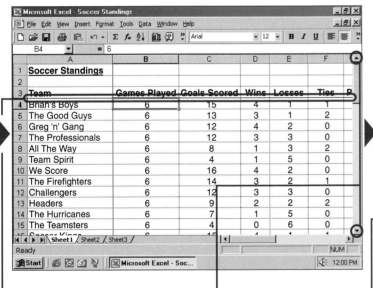

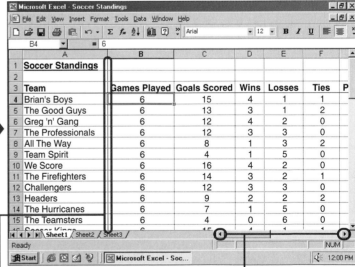

■ A horizontal line appears in your worksheet.

■ The rows above the horizontal line are frozen. These rows remain on your screen as you move through your worksheet.

■ To move through the rows below the horizontal line, click ▲ or ▼.

■ A vertical line appears in your worksheet.

■ The columns to the left of the vertical line are frozen. These columns remain on your screen as you move through your worksheet.

■ To move through the columns to the right of the vertical line, click ◀ or ▶.

SPLIT A WORKSHEET

You can split your worksheet into separate sections. This allows you to display different areas of a large worksheet at the same time.

SPLIT A WORKSHEET VERTICALLY

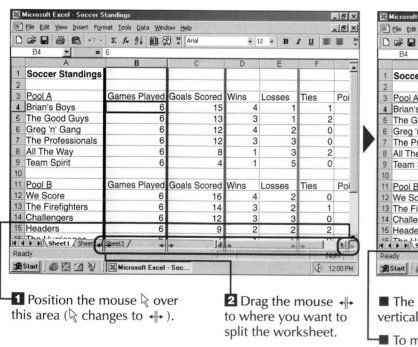

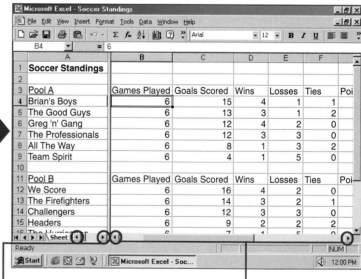

1 Position the mouse ⬡ over this area (⬡ changes to ↔).

2 Drag the mouse ↔ to where you want to split the worksheet.

■ The worksheet splits vertically into two sections.

■ To move through the columns to the left of the dividing line, click ◀ or ▶.

■ To move through the columns to the right of the dividing line, click ◀ or ▶.

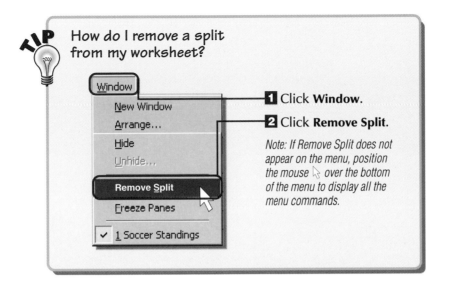

TIP

How do I remove a split
from my worksheet?

Window

New Window
Arrange...
Hide
Unhide...

Remove Split
Freeze Panes

✓ 1 Soccer Standings

1 Click **Window**.

2 Click **Remove Split**.

*Note: If Remove Split does not
appear on the menu, position
the mouse ⟨⟩ over the bottom
of the menu to display all the
menu commands.*

SPLIT A WORKSHEET HORIZONTALLY

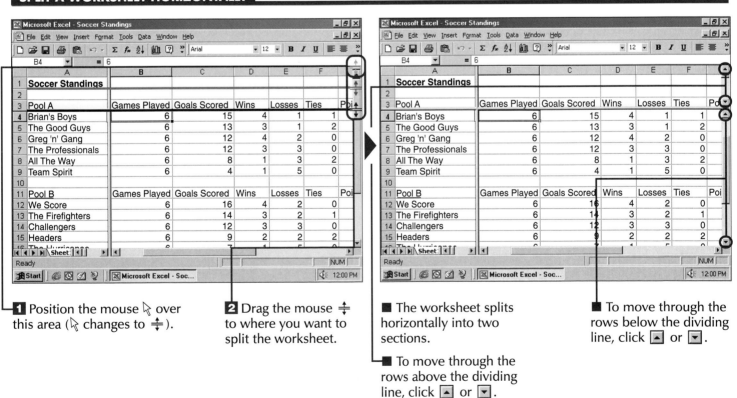

1 Position the mouse ⟨⟩ over
this area (⟨⟩ changes to ÷).

2 Drag the mouse ÷
to where you want to
split the worksheet.

■ The worksheet splits
horizontally into two
sections.

■ To move through the
rows above the dividing
line, click ▲ or ▼.

■ To move through the
rows below the dividing
line, click ▲ or ▼.

CHAPTER 6

FORMAT YOUR WORKSHEETS

Would you like to improve the appearance of your worksheet? This chapter shows you how to change the width of columns, add borders to cells, change the color of data and much more.

Change Column Width 98

Change Row Height 99

Change Font of Data 100

Change Size of Data 101

Bold, Italicize or Underline Data 102

Change Alignment of Data 103

Change Appearance of Data 104

Change Cell or Data Color 108

Add Borders 110

Clear Formatting 111

Change Number Format 112

Indent Data .116

Center Data Across Columns 117

Wrap Text in Cells 118

Rotate Data in Cells 120

Copy Formatting 122

Apply an AutoFormat 124

CHANGE COLUMN WIDTH

You can improve the appearance of your worksheet by changing the width of columns.

If a column is not wide enough to display all the data in a cell, Excel may hide part of the data. Changing the column width allows you to display the hidden data.

CHANGE COLUMN WIDTH

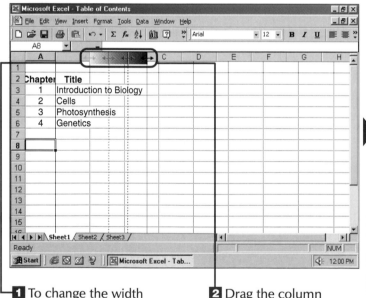

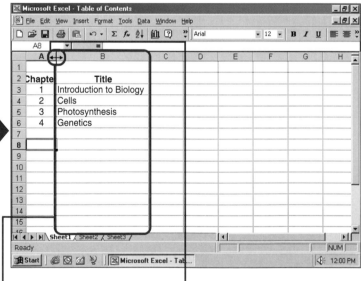

1 To change the width of a column, position the mouse ⇩ over the right edge of the column heading (⇩ changes to ↔).

2 Drag the column edge until the dotted line displays the column width you want.

■ The column displays the new width.

FIT LONGEST ITEM

You can have Excel change a column width to fit the longest item in the column.

1 Double-click the right edge of the column heading.

CHANGE ROW HEIGHT

You can change the height of rows to increase the space between the rows of data in your worksheet. This can help make the data easier to read.

CHANGE ROW HEIGHT

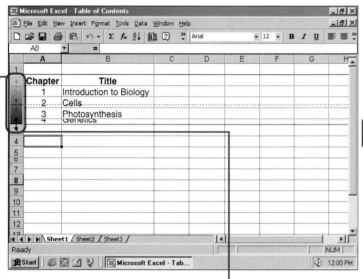

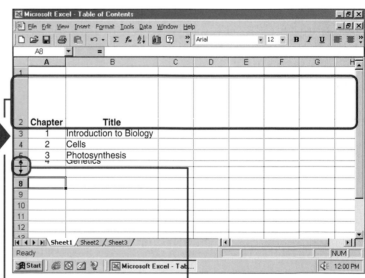

1 To change the height of a row, position the mouse ⬦ over the bottom edge of the row heading (⬦ changes to ✛).

2 Drag the row edge until the dotted line displays the row height you want.

■ The row displays the new height.

FIT TALLEST ITEM

You can have Excel change a row height to fit the tallest item in the row.

1 Double-click the bottom edge of the row heading.

CHANGE FONT OF DATA

You can enhance the appearance of your worksheet by changing the design, or font, of data.

CHANGE FONT OF DATA

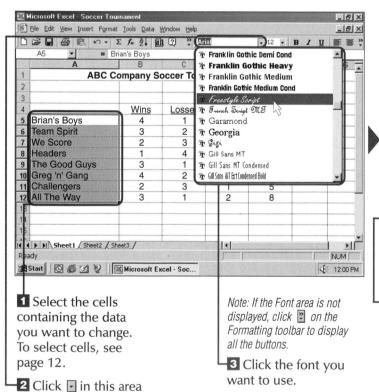

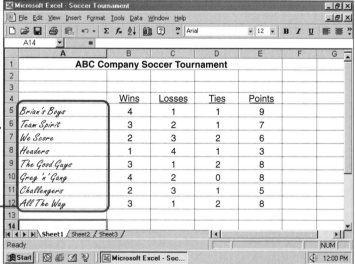

1 Select the cells containing the data you want to change. To select cells, see page 12.

2 Click ▼ in this area to display a list of the available fonts.

Note: If the Font area is not displayed, click ⟫ on the Formatting toolbar to display all the buttons.

3 Click the font you want to use.

■ The data changes to the font you selected.

■ To deselect cells, click any cell.

100

CHANGE SIZE OF DATA

You can increase or decrease the size of data in your worksheet.

Excel measures the size of data in points. There are 72 points in one inch.

CHANGE SIZE OF DATA

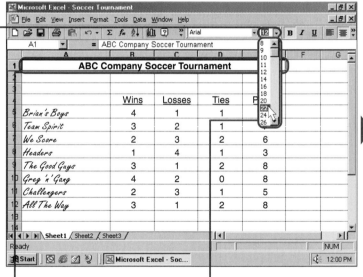

1 Select the cells containing the data you want to change. To select cells, see page 12.

2 Click ⊡ in this area to display a list of the available sizes.

Note: If the Font Size area is not displayed, click ⊠ on the Formatting toolbar to display all the buttons.

3 Click the size you want to use.

■ The data changes to the size you selected.

■ To deselect cells, click any cell.

You can use the Bold, Italic and Underline features to emphasize data in your worksheet.

BOLD, ITALICIZE OR UNDERLINE DATA

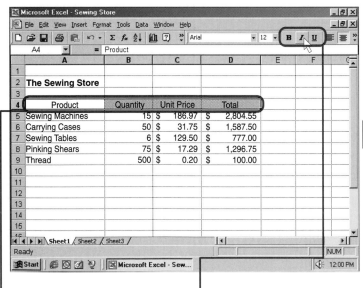

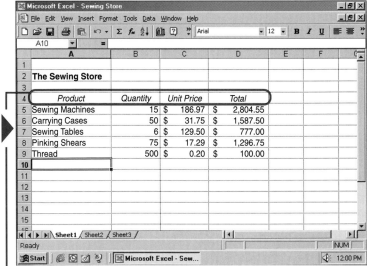

1 Select the cells containing the data you want to change. To select cells, see page 12.

2 Click one of the following buttons.

B Bold

I Italic

U Underline

Note: If the button you want is not displayed, click on the Formatting toolbar to display all the buttons.

■ The data appears in the new style.

■ To deselect cells, click any cell.

■ To remove a bold, italic or underline style, repeat steps **1** and **2**.

CHANGE ALIGNMENT OF DATA

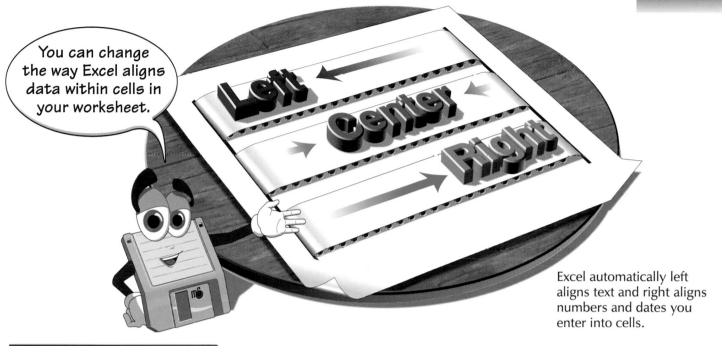

You can change the way Excel aligns data within cells in your worksheet.

Excel automatically left aligns text and right aligns numbers and dates you enter into cells.

CHANGE ALIGNMENT OF DATA

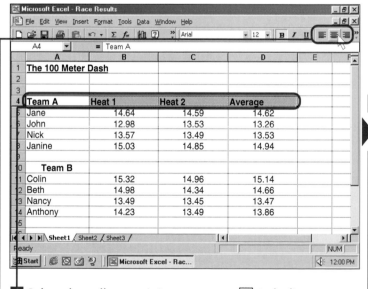

1 Select the cells containing the data you want to align differently. To select cells, see page 12.

2 Click one of these buttons.

- Left align
- Center
- Right align

Note: If the button you want is not displayed, click **»** *on the Formatting toolbar to display all the buttons.*

■ Excel aligns the data.

■ To deselect cells, click any cell.

You can make data in your worksheet look more attractive by using various fonts, styles, sizes, underlines, colors and special effects.

CHANGE APPEARANCE OF DATA

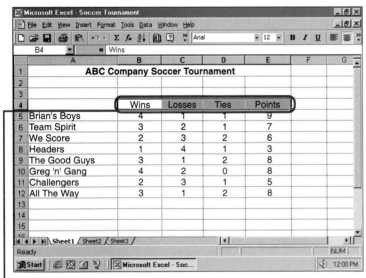

1 Select the cells containing the data you want to change. To select cells, see page 12.

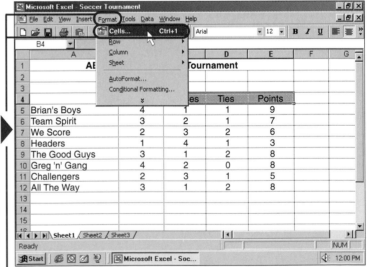

2 Click **Format**.

3 Click **Cells**.

■ The Format Cells dialog box appears.

What determines which fonts are available in Excel?

The available fonts depend on the fonts installed on your computer and printer. Excel includes several fonts, but additional fonts may be available from the other programs on your computer. Your printer may also have built-in fonts you can use.

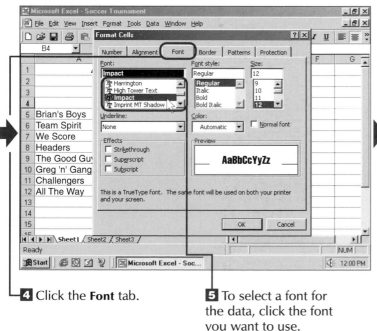

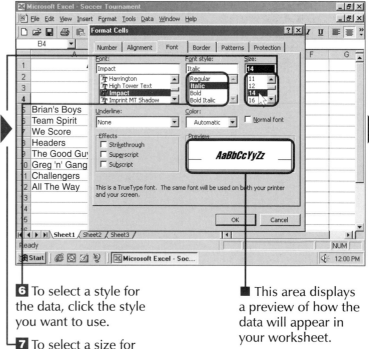

4 Click the **Font** tab.

5 To select a font for the data, click the font you want to use.

6 To select a style for the data, click the style you want to use.

7 To select a size for the data, click the size you want to use.

■ This area displays a preview of how the data will appear in your worksheet.

CONTINUED

SINGLE

SINGLE ACCOUNTING

DOUBLE

DOUBLE ACCOUNTING

Excel offers several underline styles you can use to underline data in your worksheet.

You can use underlines to emphasize the results of calculations in your worksheet.

CHANGE APPEARANCE OF DATA (CONTINUED)

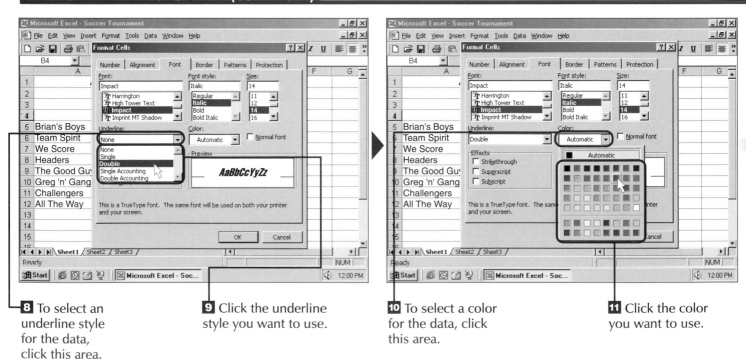

8 To select an underline style for the data, click this area.

9 Click the underline style you want to use.

10 To select a color for the data, click this area.

11 Click the color you want to use.

TIP

What effects can I add to data in my worksheet?

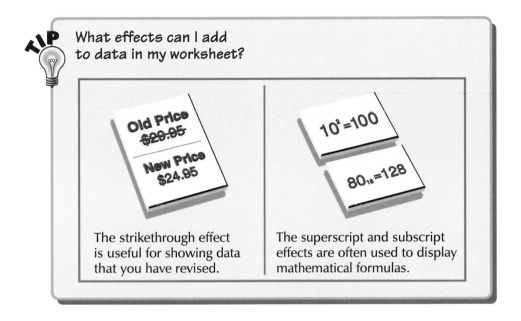

The strikethrough effect is useful for showing data that you have revised.

The superscript and subscript effects are often used to display mathematical formulas.

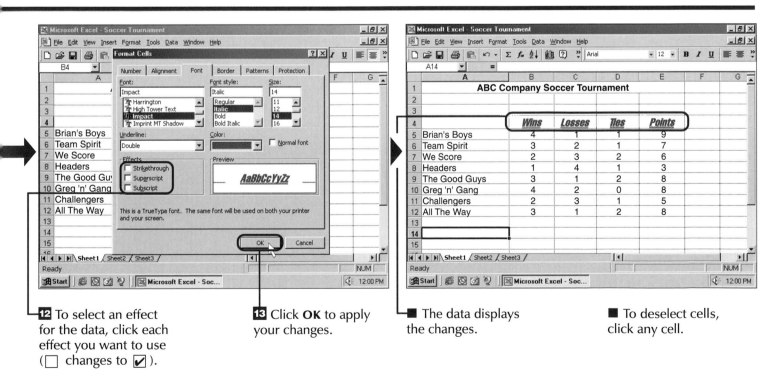

12 To select an effect for the data, click each effect you want to use (□ changes to ☑).

13 Click **OK** to apply your changes.

■ The data displays the changes.

■ To deselect cells, click any cell.

CHANGE CELL OR DATA COLOR

You can make your worksheet more attractive by adding color to cells or data.

CHANGE CELL COLOR

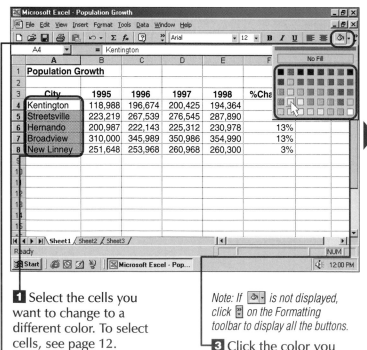

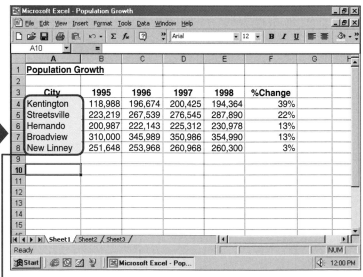

1 Select the cells you want to change to a different color. To select cells, see page 12.

2 Click ▾ in this area to select a color.

Note: If 🎨▾ is not displayed, click ≫ on the Formatting toolbar to display all the buttons.

3 Click the color you want to use.

■ The cells display the new color.

■ To deselect cells, click any cell.

■ To remove a color from cells, repeat steps 1 to 3, except select **No Fill** in step 3.

What colors should I choose?

When adding color to your worksheet, make sure you choose cell and data colors that work well together. For example, red data on a blue background is difficult to read.

CHANGE DATA COLOR

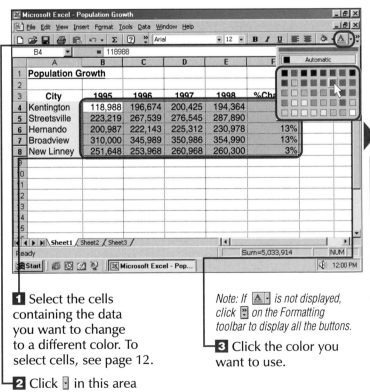

1 Select the cells containing the data you want to change to a different color. To select cells, see page 12.

2 Click ⬝ in this area to select a color.

Note: If [A]▾ *is not displayed, click* ⬝ *on the Formatting toolbar to display all the buttons.*

3 Click the color you want to use.

■ The data displays the new color.

■ To deselect cells, click any cell.

■ To remove a color from data, repeat steps **1** to **3**, except select **Automatic** in step **3**.

ADD BORDERS

You can add borders to enhance the appearance of your worksheet. You can also use borders to divide your worksheet into sections.

	Jan	Feb
Product A	1254	1998
Product B	1245	1674
Product C	1356	1678
Product D	1675	1878
Product E	1785	1563
Product F	1674	1677
Product G	1876	1784
Product H	1467	1676

ADD BORDERS

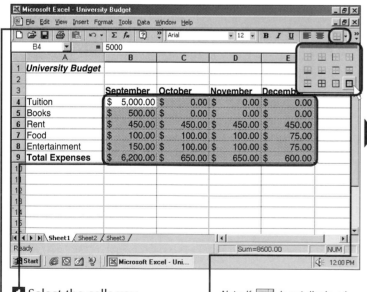

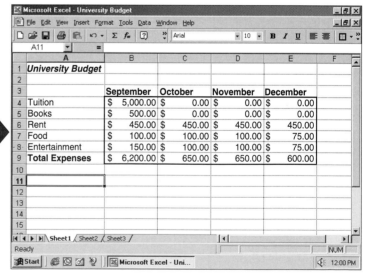

1 Select the cells you want to display borders. To select cells, see page 12.

2 Click ▥ in this area to display the types of borders you can add to the cells.

Note: If ▥ is not displayed, click ⟩⟩ on the Formatting toolbar to display all the buttons.

3 Click the type of border you want to add.

■ The cells display the border you selected.

■ To deselect cells, click any cell.

■ To remove the borders from cells, repeat steps **1** to **3**, except select ▦ in step **3**.

110

CLEAR FORMATTING

You can remove all the formatting from cells in your worksheet.

CLEAR FORMATTING

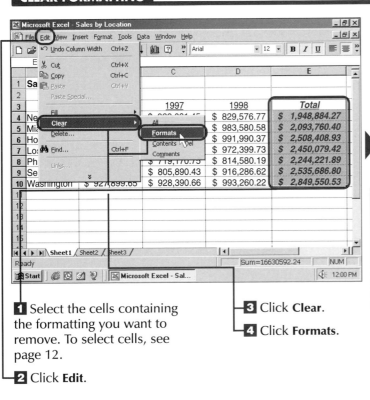

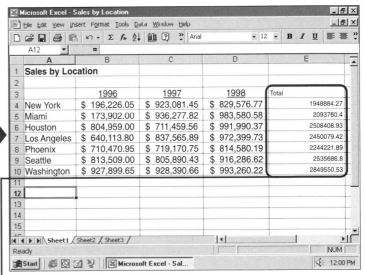

1 Select the cells containing the formatting you want to remove. To select cells, see page 12.

2 Click **Edit**.

3 Click **Clear**.

4 Click **Formats**.

■ All the formatting disappears from the cells you selected.

■ To deselect cells, click any cell.

Note: If you clear the formatting from cells containing dates, the dates change to numbers. To once again display the dates, you must change the format of the cells to the Date format. For more information, see page 114.

CHANGE NUMBER FORMAT

You can change the appearance of numbers in your worksheet without retyping the numbers.

When you change the format of numbers, you do not change the value of the numbers.

CHANGE THE NUMBER STYLE

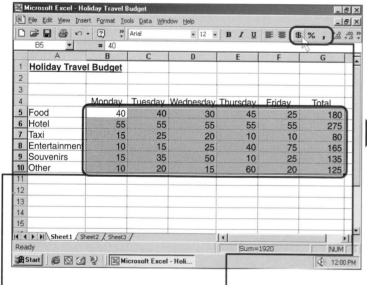

1 Select the cells containing the numbers you want to change. To select cells, see page 12.

2 Click one of the following buttons.

$ Currency

% Percent

, Comma

Note: If the button you want is not displayed, click ⟩⟩ on the Formatting toolbar to display all the buttons.

■ The numbers display the style you selected.

■ To deselect cells, click any cell.

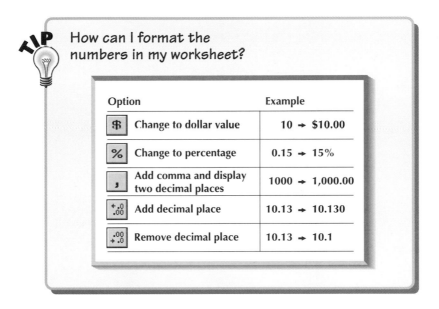

TIP

How can I format the numbers in my worksheet?

Option		Example
$	Change to dollar value	10 ➔ $10.00
%	Change to percentage	0.15 ➔ 15%
,	Add comma and display two decimal places	1000 ➔ 1,000.00
⁺.₀₀	Add decimal place	10.13 ➔ 10.130
.₀₀	Remove decimal place	10.13 ➔ 10.1

ADD OR REMOVE A DECIMAL PLACE

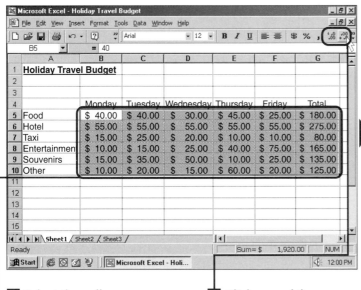

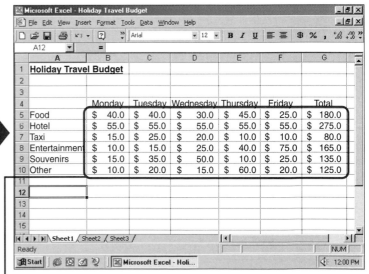

1 Select the cells containing the numbers you want to change. To select cells, see page 12.

2 Click one of the following buttons.

⁺.₀₀ Add decimal place

.₀₀ Remove decimal place

Note: If the button you want is not displayed, click ⟩⟩ on the Formatting toolbar to display all the buttons.

■ Excel increases or decreases the number of decimal places.

■ To deselect cells, click any cell.

CHANGE NUMBER FORMAT

Currency
$1,000
$1,000.00
($1,000.00)

Date
14-Mar-99
Mar-99
3/14/99
March 14, 1999

Scientific
3.456E+03
3.E+03

Excel offers many different formats that you can use to make the numbers in your worksheet easier to read.

When you change the format of numbers, you do not change the value of the numbers.

USING THE FORMAT CELLS DIALOG BOX

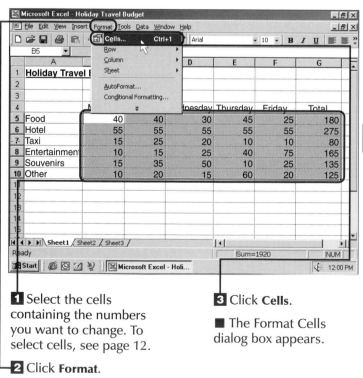

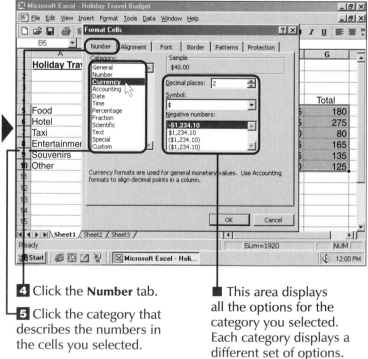

1 Select the cells containing the numbers you want to change. To select cells, see page 12.

2 Click **Format**.

3 Click **Cells**.

■ The Format Cells dialog box appears.

4 Click the **Number** tab.

5 Click the category that describes the numbers in the cells you selected.

■ This area displays all the options for the category you selected. Each category displays a different set of options.

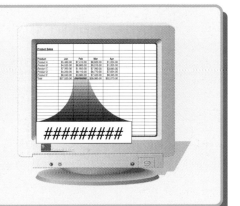

TIP

Why did number signs (#) appear in a cell after I changed the number format?

If number signs (#) appear in a cell, the column is not wide enough to display the entire number. To change the column width, see page 98.

##########

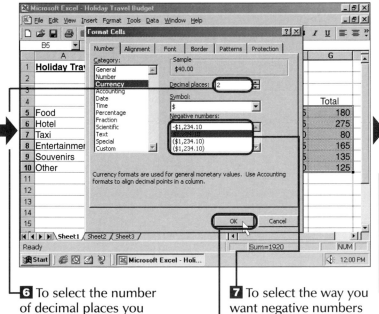

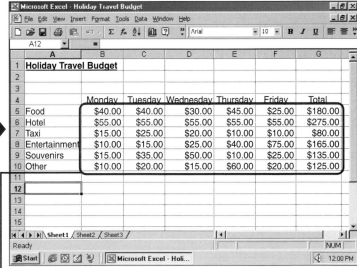

6 To select the number of decimal places you want the numbers to display, double-click this area. Then type the number of decimal places.

7 To select the way you want negative numbers to appear, click one of the available styles.

8 Click **OK** to apply your changes.

■ The numbers display the changes.

■ To deselect cells, click any cell.

INDENT DATA

You can indent data to move the data away from the left edge of a cell.

INDENT DATA

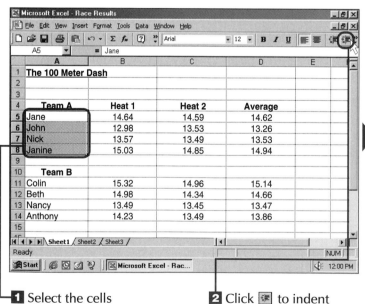

1 Select the cells containing the data you want to indent. To select cells, see page 12.

2 Click 🔳 to indent the data.

Note: If 🔳 is not displayed, click 🔛 on the Formatting toolbar to display all the buttons.

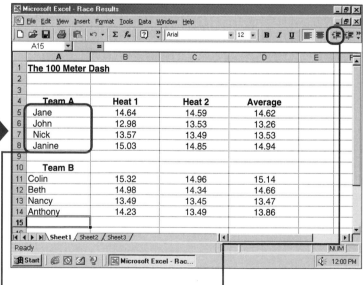

■ Excel indents the data.

■ To deselect cells, click any cell.

■ To remove the indent, repeat steps **1** and **2**, except click 🔳 in step **2**.

Note: If 🔳 is not displayed, click 🔛 on the Formatting toolbar to display all the buttons.

116

CENTER DATA ACROSS COLUMNS

You can center data across several columns in your worksheet. This is useful for centering titles over your data.

CENTER DATA ACROSS COLUMNS

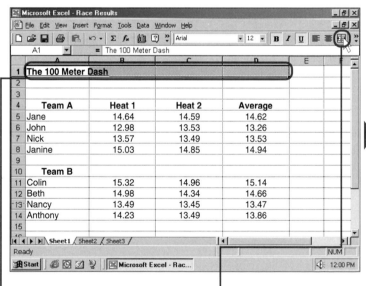

1 Select the cells you want to center the data across. To select cells, see page 12.

Note: The first cell you select should contain the data you want to center.

2 Click 🖽 to center the data.

Note: If 🖽 is not displayed, click ⟩⟩ on the Formatting toolbar to display all the buttons.

■ Excel centers the data across the cells you selected.

WRAP TEXT IN CELLS

You can display long lines of text within cells by wrapping the text.

WRAP TEXT IN CELLS

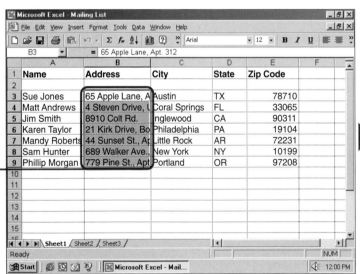

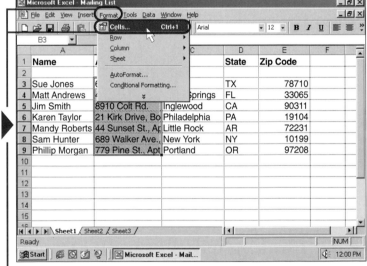

1 Select the cells containing the text you want to wrap. To select cells, see page 12.

2 Click **Format**.

3 Click **Cells**.

■ The Format Cells dialog box appears.

Can I display all the text in a cell without wrapping the text?

You can have Excel reduce the size of text to fit within a cell. Perform steps **1** to **6** below, except select **Shrink to fit** in step **5** (☐ changes to ☑).

If you later change the width of the column, Excel will automatically adjust the size of the text to fit the new width.

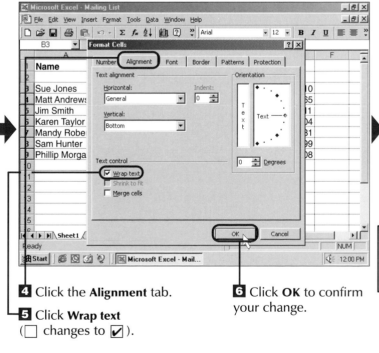

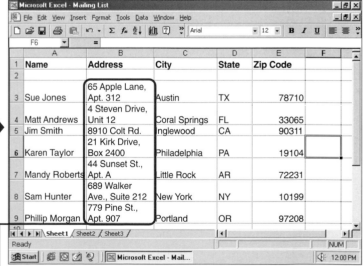

4 Click the **Alignment** tab.

5 Click **Wrap text** (☐ changes to ☑).

6 Click **OK** to confirm your change.

■ The text wraps within the cells you selected. The row heights change to fit the wrapped text.

■ To deselect cells, click any cell.

You can rotate data within cells in your worksheet. This is useful for emphasizing row and column labels.

ROTATE DATA IN CELLS

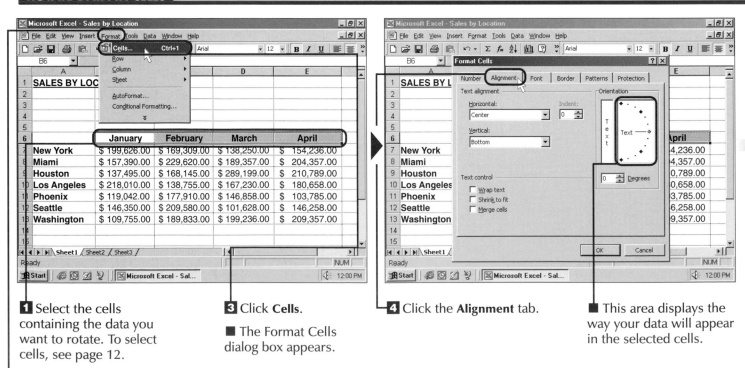

1 Select the cells containing the data you want to rotate. To select cells, see page 12.

2 Click **Format**.

3 Click **Cells**.

■ The Format Cells dialog box appears.

4 Click the **Alignment** tab.

■ This area displays the way your data will appear in the selected cells.

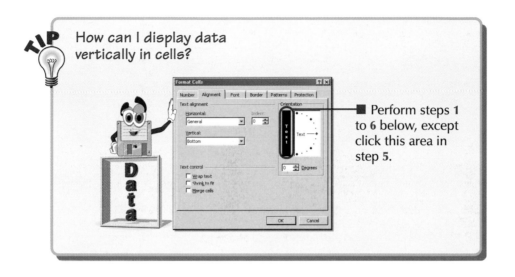

How can I display data vertically in cells?

■ Perform steps **1** to **6** below, except click this area in step **5**.

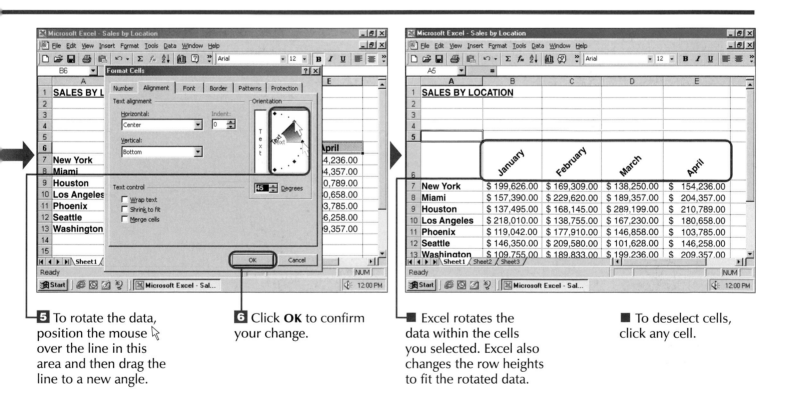

5 To rotate the data, position the mouse ☝ over the line in this area and then drag the line to a new angle.

6 Click **OK** to confirm your change.

■ Excel rotates the data within the cells you selected. Excel also changes the row heights to fit the rotated data.

■ To deselect cells, click any cell.

Once you format one cell to suit your needs, you can make other cells look exactly the same.

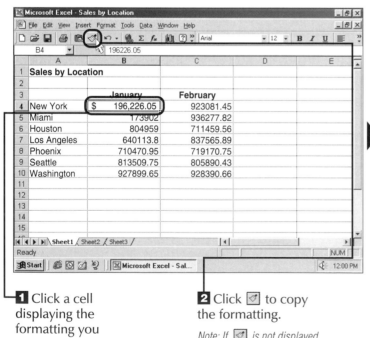

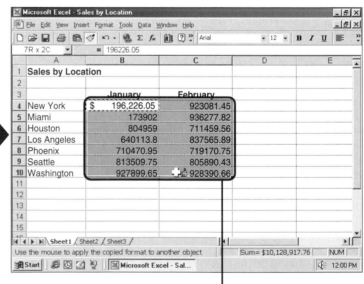

1 Click a cell displaying the formatting you want to copy.

2 Click to copy the formatting.

Note: If is not displayed, click on the Standard toolbar to display all the buttons.

■ The mouse changes to when over your worksheet.

3 Select the cells you want to display the formatting. To select cells, see page 12.

122

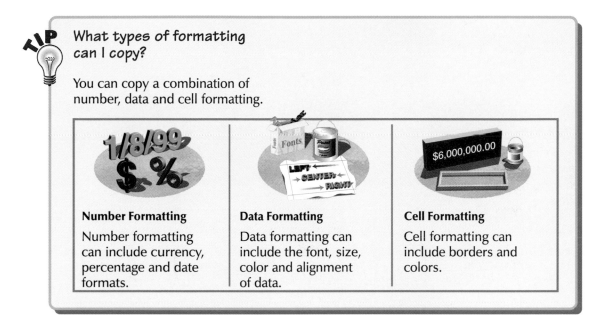

TIP

**What types of formatting
can I copy?**

You can copy a combination of
number, data and cell formatting.

Number Formatting

Number formatting
can include currency,
percentage and date
formats.

Data Formatting

Data formatting can
include the font, size,
color and alignment
of data.

Cell Formatting

Cell formatting can
include borders and
colors.

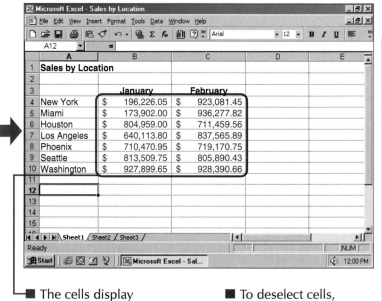

■ The cells display
the formatting.

■ To deselect cells,
click any cell.

**COPY FORMATTING
TO SEVERAL AREAS**

1 Click a cell displaying
the formatting you want
to copy.

2 Double-click 🖌 to
copy the formatting.

*Note: If 🖌 is not displayed,
click ⏵ on the Standard toolbar
to display all the buttons.*

3 Select each group of
cells you want to display
the formatting.

4 When you finish
copying the formatting,
press the Esc key.

Excel offers many ready-to-use designs, called AutoFormats, that you can choose from to give your worksheet a new appearance.

APPLY AN AUTOFORMAT

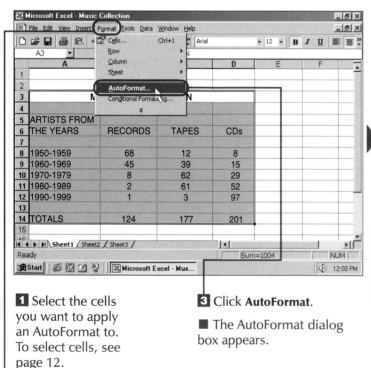

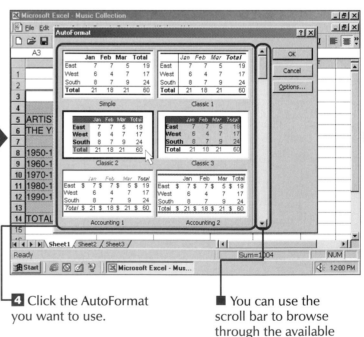

1 Select the cells you want to apply an AutoFormat to. To select cells, see page 12.

2 Click **Format**.

3 Click **AutoFormat**.

■ The AutoFormat dialog box appears.

4 Click the AutoFormat you want to use.

■ You can use the scroll bar to browse through the available AutoFormats.

**What formatting does an
AutoFormat include?**

Each AutoFormat includes a
combination of formats, such
as text and number styles,
fonts, colors and borders
that you can use to create a
professional-looking worksheet.

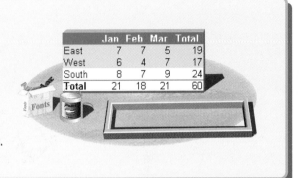

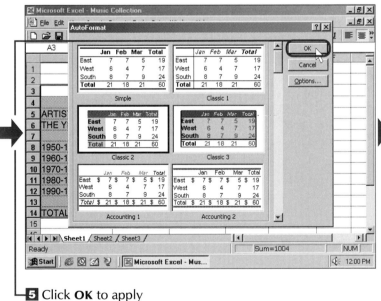

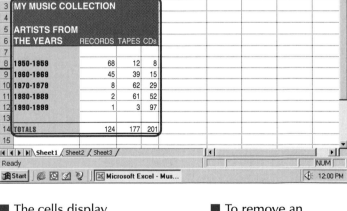

5 Click **OK** to apply
the AutoFormat to the
cells you selected.

■ The cells display
the AutoFormat you
selected.

■ To deselect cells,
click any cell.

■ To remove an
AutoFormat, repeat
steps **1** to **5**, except
select **None** in step **4**.

CHAPTER 7

PRINT YOUR WORKSHEETS

Are you ready to print your worksheet? In this chapter you will learn how to preview your worksheet and change the way your worksheet appears on a printed page.

Preview a Worksheet 128

Print a Worksheet 130

Set a Print Area 132

Center Data on a Page 134

Change Page Orientation 135

Change Margins 136

Change Print Options 138

Insert a Page Break 140

Add a Header or Footer 142

Change Size of Printed Data 144

Repeat Labels on Printed Pages 146

You can use the Print Preview feature to see how your worksheet will look when printed.

Previewing a worksheet lets you confirm the worksheet will print the way you want.

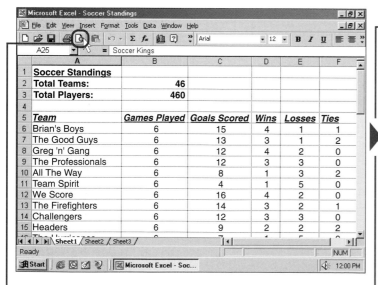

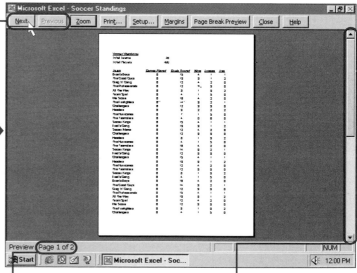

1 Click 🔍 to preview your worksheet.

Note: If 🔍 is not displayed, click ≫ on the Standard toolbar to display all the buttons.

■ The Print Preview window appears.

■ This area indicates which page is displayed and the total number of pages in your worksheet.

2 If your worksheet contains more than one page, you can click **Next** or **Previous** to view the next or previous page.

■ You can also use the scroll bar to view other pages.

128

Why does my worksheet appear in black and white in the Print Preview window?

If you are using a black-and-white printer, your worksheet appears in black and white in the Print Preview window. If you are using a color printer, your worksheet appears in color.

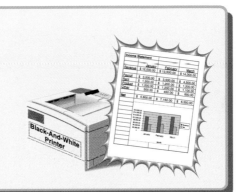

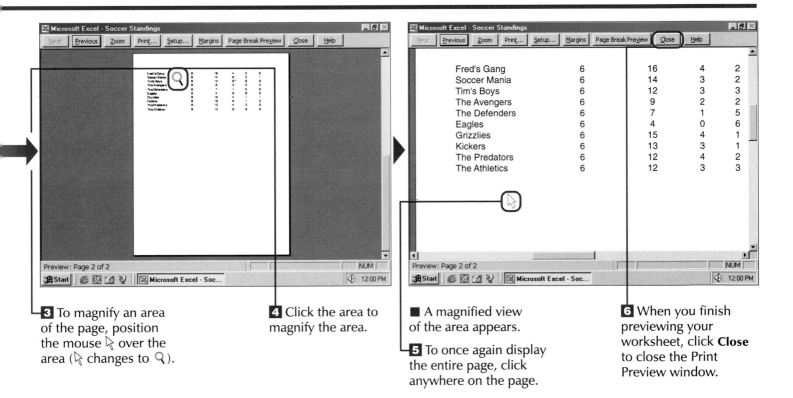

3 To magnify an area of the page, position the mouse ↕ over the area (↕ changes to ⚲).

4 Click the area to magnify the area.

■ A magnified view of the area appears.

5 To once again display the entire page, click anywhere on the page.

6 When you finish previewing your worksheet, click **Close** to close the Print Preview window.

PRINT A WORKSHEET

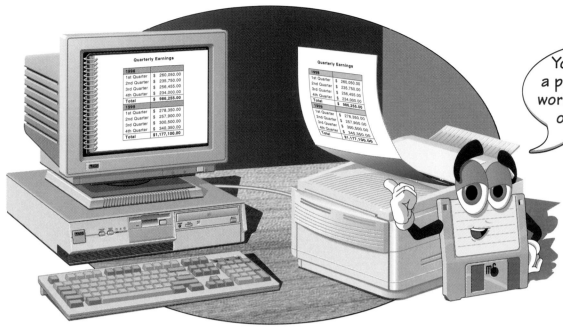

You can produce a paper copy of the worksheet displayed on your screen.

Before printing your worksheet, make sure the printer is turned on and contains an adequate supply of paper.

PRINT A WORKSHEET

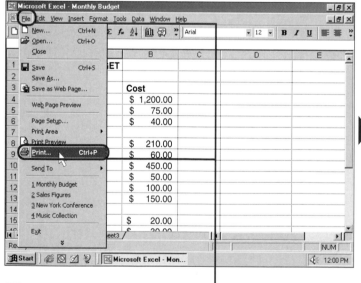

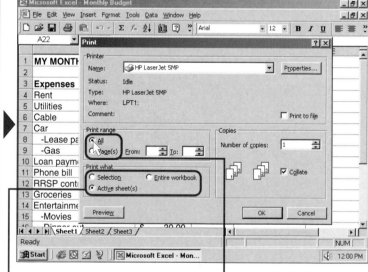

1 Click any cell in the worksheet you want to print.

■ To print only specific cells in the worksheet, select the cells you want to print. To select cells, see page 12.

2 Click **File**.

3 Click **Print**.

■ The Print dialog box appears.

4 Click the part of the workbook you want to print (○ changes to ⊙).

5 If the part of the workbook you selected to print contains more than one page, click an option to specify which pages you want to print (○ changes to ⊙).

130

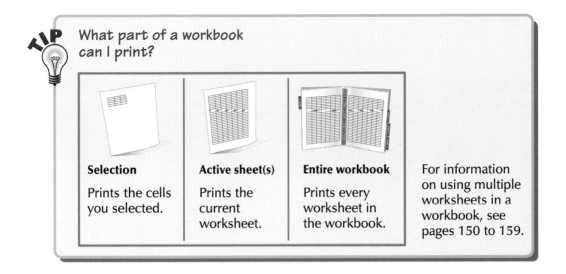

TIP

What part of a workbook can I print?

Selection

Prints the cells you selected.

Active sheet(s)

Prints the current worksheet.

Entire workbook

Prints every worksheet in the workbook.

For information on using multiple worksheets in a workbook, see pages 150 to 159.

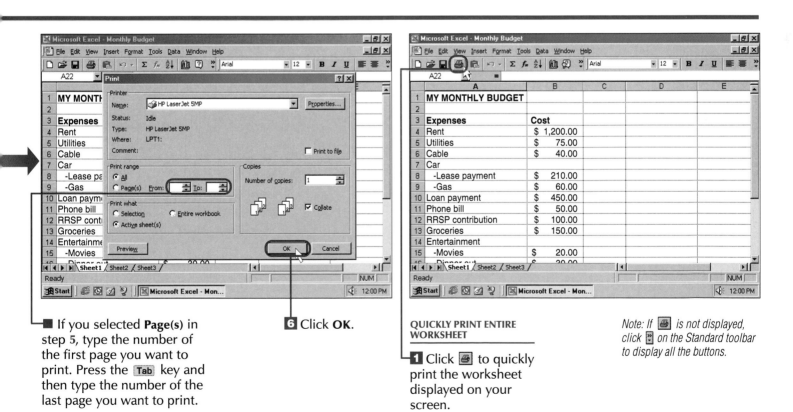

■ If you selected **Page(s)** in step 5, type the number of the first page you want to print. Press the Tab key and then type the number of the last page you want to print.

6 Click **OK**.

QUICKLY PRINT ENTIRE WORKSHEET

1 Click 🖨 to quickly print the worksheet displayed on your screen.

Note: If 🖨 is not displayed, click ≫ on the Standard toolbar to display all the buttons.

SET A PRINT AREA

If you always print the same area of your worksheet, you can set a print area to quickly print the data. Excel will print only the data in the print area.

If you have not set a print area for your worksheet, Excel will print the entire worksheet.

SET A PRINT AREA

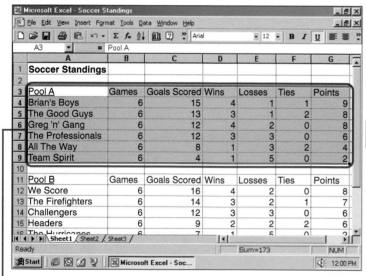

1 Select the cells containing the data you want to include in the print area. To select cells, see page 12.

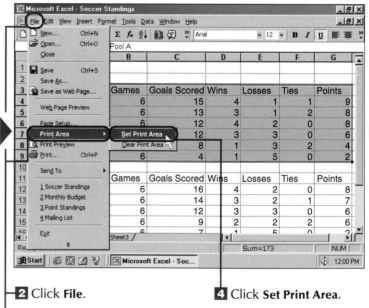

2 Click **File**.

3 Click **Print Area**.

4 Click **Set Print Area**.

How do I print other data in my worksheet after I set a print area?

You can temporarily override a print area you have set and print other data in your worksheet. Select the cells containing the data you want to print and then perform steps **2** to **6** starting on page 130, choosing **Selection** in step **4** (○ changes to ⊙).

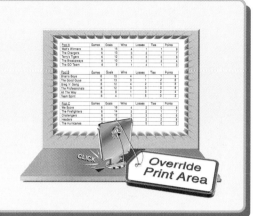

CLICK

Override
Print Area

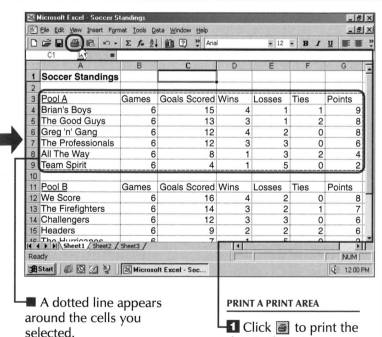

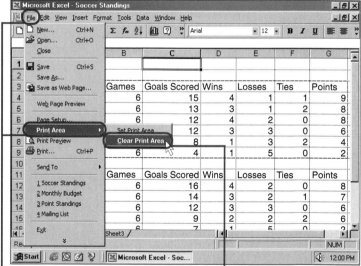

■ A dotted line appears around the cells you selected.

■ To deselect cells, click any cell.

PRINT A PRINT AREA

1 Click 🖨 to print the data in the print area at any time.

CLEAR A PRINT AREA

1 Click **File**.

2 Click **Print Area**.

3 Click **Clear Print Area** to clear the print area from your worksheet.

■ The dotted line disappears from your worksheet.

You can center data horizontally and vertically between the margins on a page.

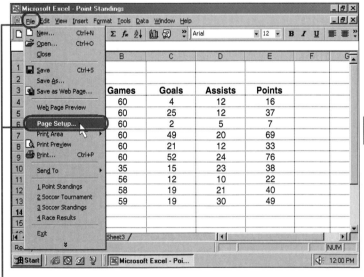

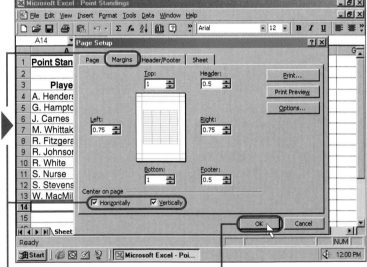

1 Click **File**.

2 Click **Page Setup**.

■ The Page Setup dialog box appears.

3 Click the **Margins** tab.

4 Click the way you want to center the data (☐ changes to ☑). You can select both center options if you wish.

5 Click **OK** to confirm your change.

Note: Centering data on a page changes the way your worksheet appears on a printed page, but does not affect the way the worksheet appears on your screen.

134

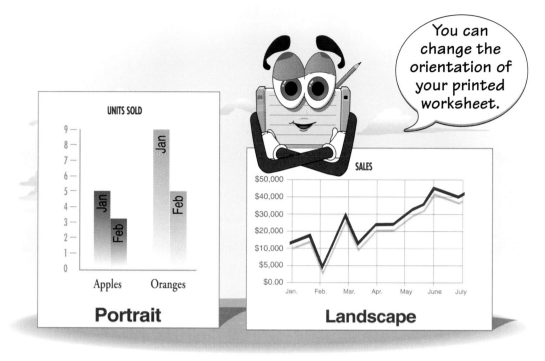

Excel automatically prints worksheets in the portrait orientation. The landscape orientation is useful when you want a wide worksheet to fit on one printed page.

CHANGE PAGE ORIENTATION

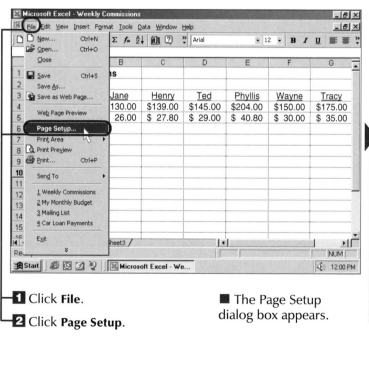

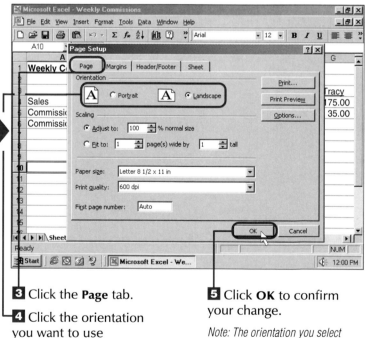

1 Click **File**.

2 Click **Page Setup**.

■ The Page Setup dialog box appears.

3 Click the **Page** tab.

4 Click the orientation you want to use (○ changes to ⊙).

5 Click **OK** to confirm your change.

Note: The orientation you select changes the way your worksheet appears on a printed page, but does not affect the way the worksheet appears on your screen.

CHANGE MARGINS

A margin is the amount of space between data and an edge of your paper. You can change the margins for your worksheet.

Excel automatically sets the top and bottom margins to 1 inch and the left and right margins to 0.75 inches.

CHANGE MARGINS

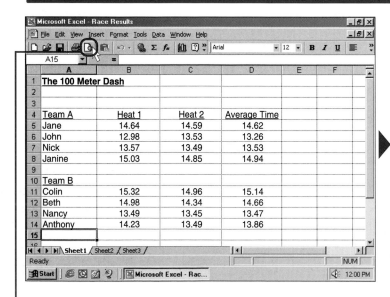

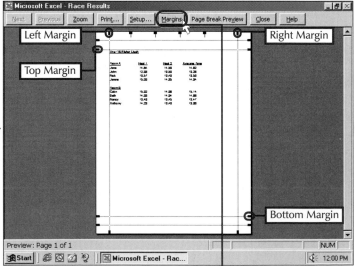

1 Click 🔍 to display your worksheet in the Print Preview window. This window allows you to change the margins.

Note: If 🔍 is not displayed, click 🔀 on the Standard toolbar to display all the buttons.

■ The worksheet appears in the Print Preview window.

Note: For information on the Print Preview feature, see page 128.

2 If the margins are not displayed, click **Margins**.

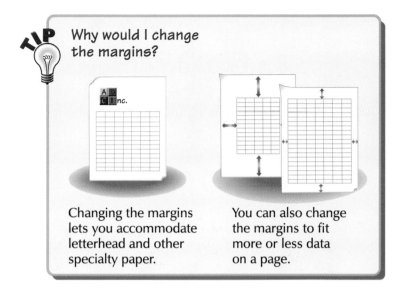

**Why would I change
the margins?**

Changing the margins
lets you accommodate
letterhead and other
specialty paper.

You can also change
the margins to fit
more or less data
on a page.

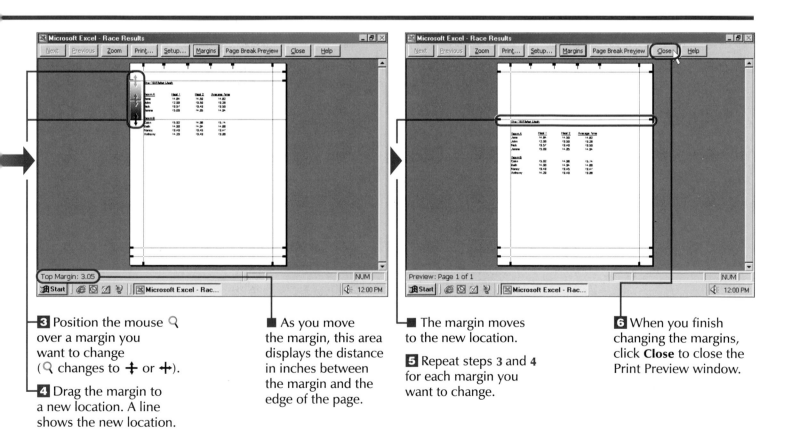

3 Position the mouse Q
over a margin you
want to change
(Q changes to ✛ or ✛).

4 Drag the margin to
a new location. A line
shows the new location.

■ As you move
the margin, this area
displays the distance
in inches between
the margin and the
edge of the page.

■ The margin moves
to the new location.

5 Repeat steps **3** and **4**
for each margin you
want to change.

6 When you finish
changing the margins,
click **Close** to close the
Print Preview window.

Excel offers several print options that let you change the way your worksheet appears on a printed page.

CHANGE PRINT OPTIONS

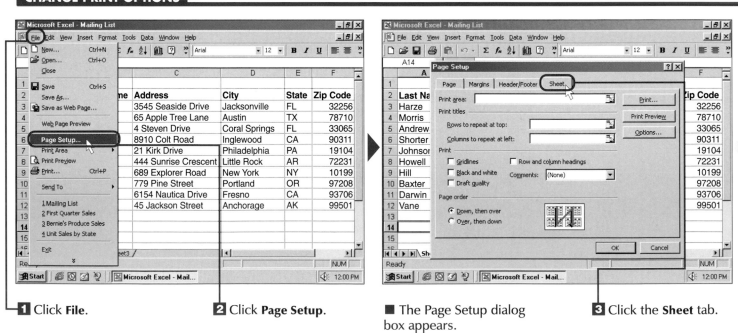

1 Click **File**.

2 Click **Page Setup**.

■ The Page Setup dialog box appears.

3 Click the **Sheet** tab.

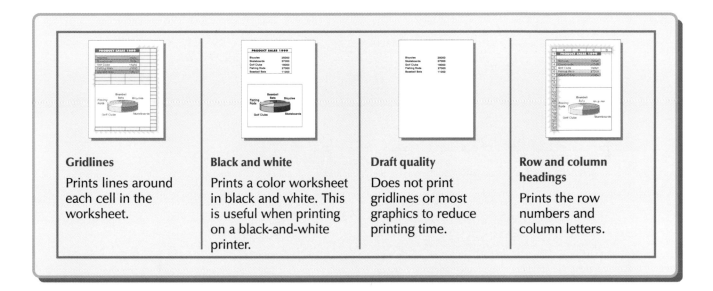

Gridlines

Prints lines around
each cell in the
worksheet.

Black and white

Prints a color worksheet
in black and white. This
is useful when printing
on a black-and-white
printer.

Draft quality

Does not print
gridlines or most
graphics to reduce
printing time.

**Row and column
headings**

Prints the row
numbers and
column letters.

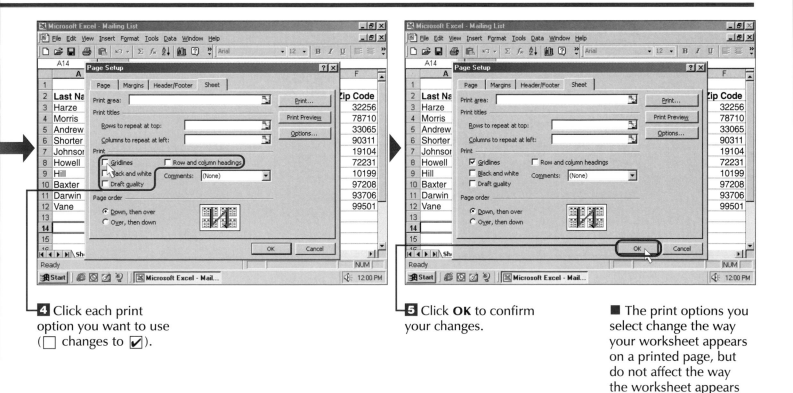

4 Click each print
option you want to use
(☐ changes to ☑).

5 Click **OK** to confirm
your changes.

■ The print options you
select change the way
your worksheet appears
on a printed page, but
do not affect the way
the worksheet appears
on your screen.

You can insert a page break when you want to start a new page at a specific place in your worksheet. A page break indicates where one page ends and another begins.

INSERT A PAGE BREAK

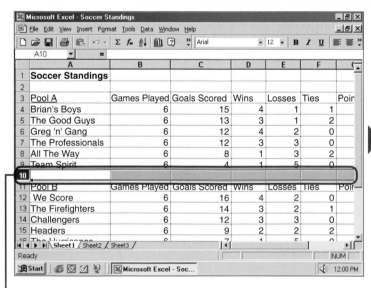

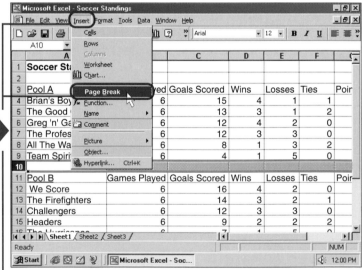

1 To select the row or column you want to appear at the beginning of the new page, click the heading of the row or column.

2 Click **Insert**.

3 Click **Page Break**.

Note: If Page Break does not appear on the menu, position the mouse over the bottom of the menu to display all the menu commands.

Will Excel ever insert page breaks automatically?

When you fill a page with data, Excel automatically starts a new page by inserting a page break for you.

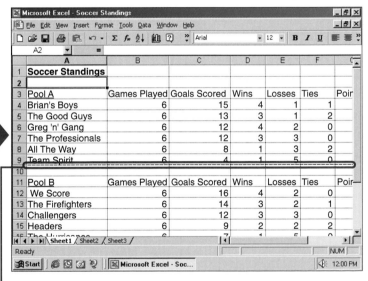

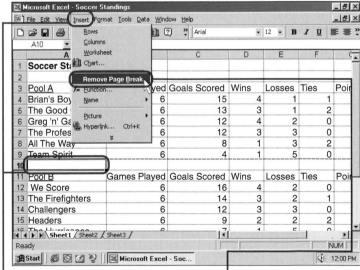

■ A dotted line appears on your screen. This line indicates where one page ends and another begins. The dotted line will not appear when you print your worksheet.

■ To deselect a row or column, click any cell.

DELETE A PAGE BREAK

1 Click a cell directly below or directly to the right of the page break line you want to delete.

2 Click **Insert**.

3 Click **Remove Page Break** to remove the page break.

■ The dotted line disappears from your worksheet.

ADD A HEADER OR FOOTER

You can add a header or footer to every page of your worksheet. A header or footer can contain information such as your name, the page number and the current date.

■ A header appears at the top of each printed page.

■ A footer appears at the bottom of each printed page.

ADD A HEADER OR FOOTER

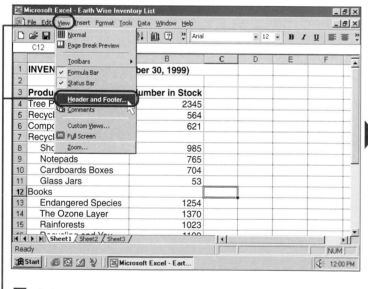

1 Click **View**.

2 Click **Header and Footer**.

Note: If Header and Footer does not appear on the menu, position the mouse ☒ over the bottom of the menu to display all the menu commands.

■ The Page Setup dialog box appears.

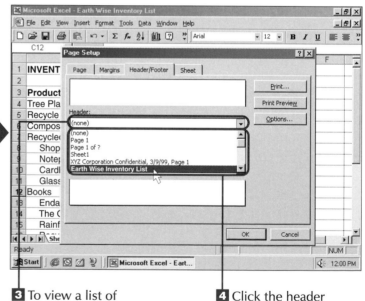

3 To view a list of headers you can use, click this area.

4 Click the header you want to use.

**Can I see how a header
or footer will look before
I print my worksheet?**

You can use the Print Preview
feature to view a header or
footer on your worksheet
before you print the worksheet.
For information on the Print
Preview feature, see page 128.

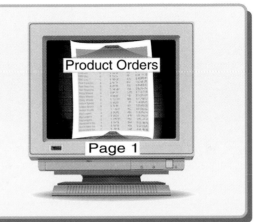

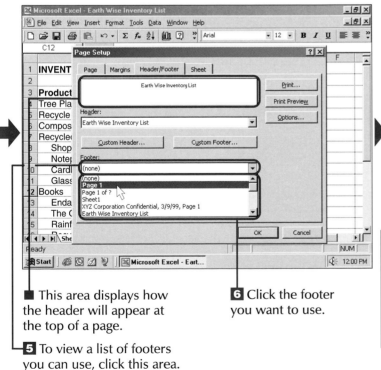

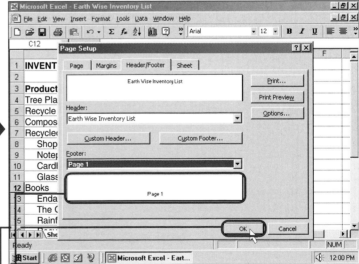

■ This area displays how
the header will appear at
the top of a page.

5 To view a list of footers
you can use, click this area.

6 Click the footer
you want to use.

■ This area displays how
the footer will appear at
the bottom of a page.

7 Click **OK** to add the
header or footer to your
worksheet.

■ To remove a header
or footer from your
worksheet, repeat
steps **1** to **7**, except
select **(none)** in step **4**
or step **6**.

CHANGE SIZE OF PRINTED DATA

You can reduce the size of printed data to print your worksheet on a specific number of pages.

Changing the size of printed data is useful when the last page of your worksheet contains a small amount of data that you want to fit on the previous page.

CHANGE SIZE OF PRINTED DATA

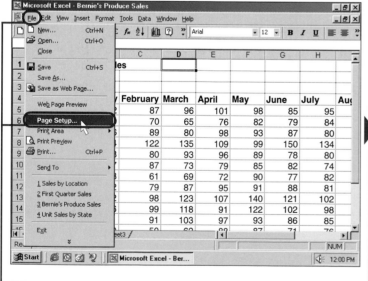

1 Click **File**.

2 Click **Page Setup**.

■ The Page Setup dialog box appears.

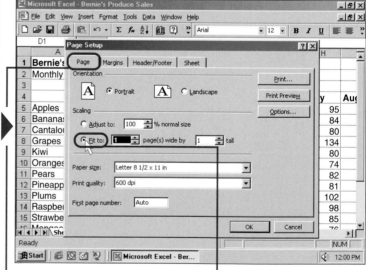

3 Click the **Page** tab.

4 Click **Fit to** to fit the worksheet on a specific number of pages (○ changes to ⦿).

TIP

What information does Excel require to change the size of my printed data?

To change the size of printed data, you must specify how many pages you want the data to print across and down.

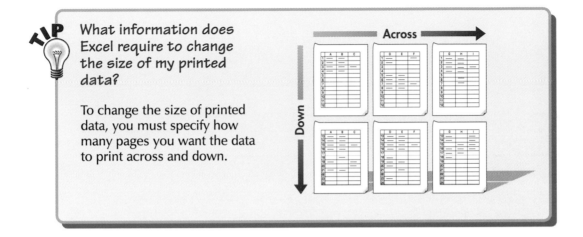

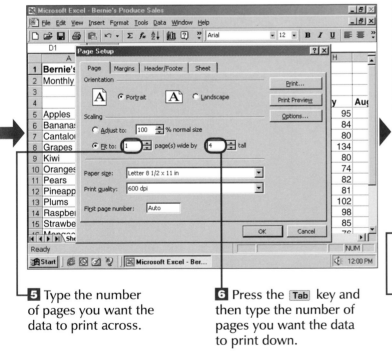

5 Type the number of pages you want the data to print across.

6 Press the `Tab` key and then type the number of pages you want the data to print down.

7 Click **OK** to confirm your changes.

■ Excel will change the size of the printed data to fit on the number of pages you specified.

■ Changing the size of printed data affects the way your worksheet appears when printed, but does not affect the way the worksheet appears on your screen.

You can display the same row or column labels on every printed page. This can help you review worksheets that print on more than one page.

Repeat a Row

Repeat a Column

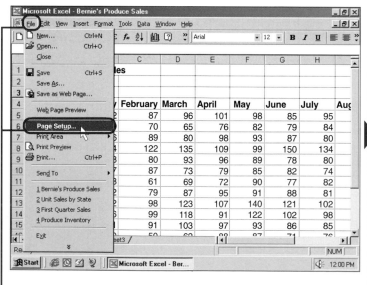

1 Click **File**.

2 Click **Page Setup**.

■ The Page Setup dialog box appears.

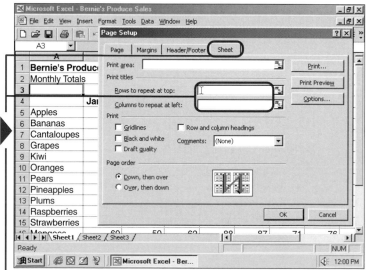

3 Click the **Sheet** tab.

4 Click the area beside one of these options.

Rows to repeat at top

Repeat labels across top of each page

Columns to repeat at left

Repeat labels down left side of each page

How can I see the repeated labels on my screen?

The repeated row or column labels will only appear when you print your worksheet. The labels will not be repeated on your screen. You can use the Print Preview feature to see how the repeated labels will look when you print your worksheet. For information on the Print Preview feature, see page 128.

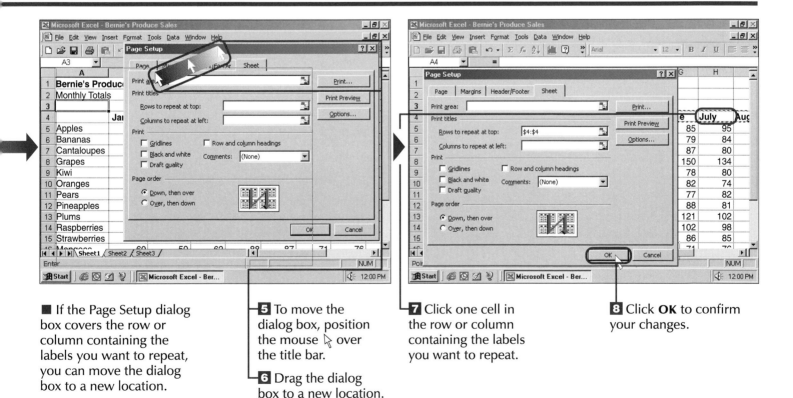

■ If the Page Setup dialog box covers the row or column containing the labels you want to repeat, you can move the dialog box to a new location.

5 To move the dialog box, position the mouse over the title bar.

6 Drag the dialog box to a new location.

7 Click one cell in the row or column containing the labels you want to repeat.

8 Click **OK** to confirm your changes.

CHAPTER 8

WORK WITH MULTIPLE WORKSHEETS

Do you want to work with more than one worksheet at a time? This chapter teaches you how to switch between worksheets, move or copy data between worksheets and more.

Switch Between Worksheets 150

Insert a Worksheet 152

Delete a Worksheet 153

Rename a Worksheet 154

Move a Worksheet 155

Move or Copy Data Between Worksheets . .156

Enter a Formula Across Worksheets 158

SWITCH BETWEEN WORKSHEETS

The worksheet displayed on your screen is one of several worksheets in your workbook. You can easily switch from one worksheet to another.

SWITCH BETWEEN WORKSHEETS

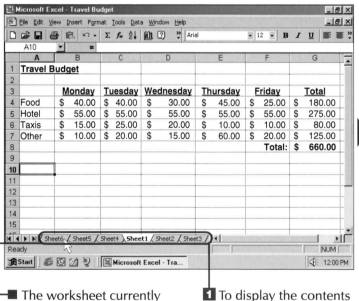

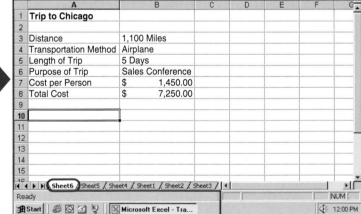

■ The worksheet currently displayed on your screen has a white tab.

■ The other worksheets in the workbook have gray tabs. The contents of these worksheets are hidden.

1 To display the contents of a worksheet, click the tab of the worksheet.

■ The contents of the worksheet appear.

■ The worksheet you selected now displays a white tab.

Why would I need more than one worksheet?

Worksheets can help you organize information in your workbook. For example, you can store information for each division of a company on a separate worksheet.

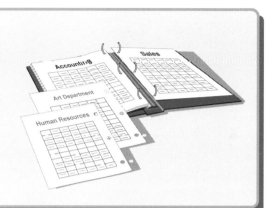

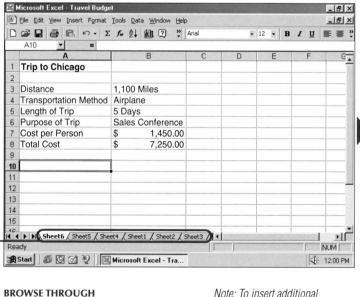

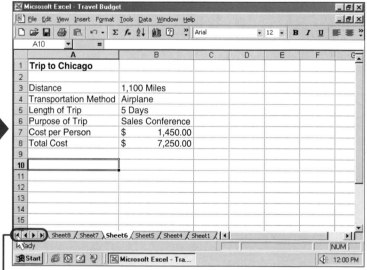

BROWSE THROUGH WORKSHEET TABS

■ If you have many worksheets in your workbook, you may not be able to see all the tabs in this area.

Note: To insert additional worksheets, see page 152.

1 Click one of these buttons to browse through the tabs.

|◄| Display first tab

|◄| Display tab to the left

|►| Display tab to the right

|►| Display last tab

You can insert a new worksheet to add related information to your workbook.

Each workbook you create automatically contains three worksheets. You can insert as many new worksheets as you need.

INSERT A WORKSHEET

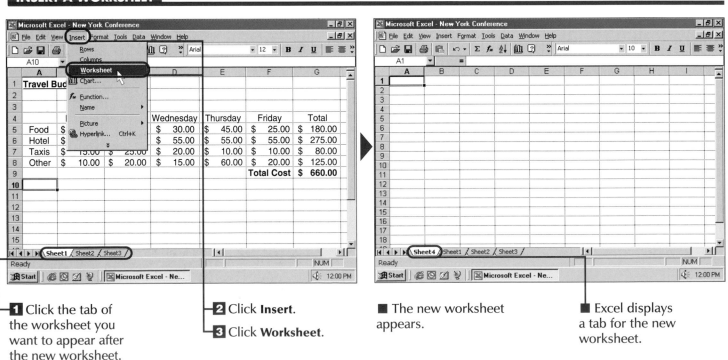

1 Click the tab of the worksheet you want to appear after the new worksheet.

2 Click **Insert**.

3 Click **Worksheet**.

■ The new worksheet appears.

■ Excel displays a tab for the new worksheet.

You can permanently remove a worksheet you no longer need from your workbook.

DELETE A WORKSHEET

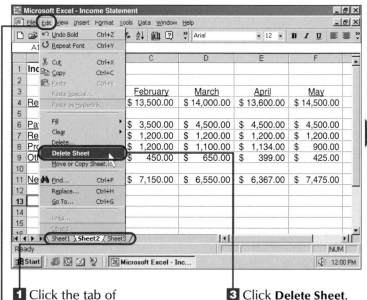

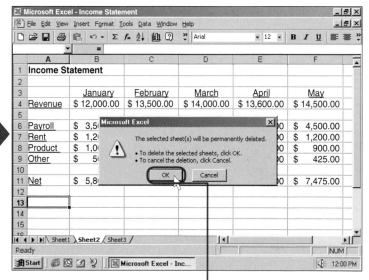

1 Click the tab of the worksheet you want to delete.

2 Click **Edit**.

3 Click **Delete Sheet**.

Note: If Delete Sheet does not appear on the menu, position the mouse ⃝ over the bottom of the menu to display all the menu commands.

■ A warning dialog box appears.

4 Click **OK** to permanently delete the worksheet.

RENAME A WORKSHEET

You can give each worksheet in your workbook a descriptive name. Descriptive names can help you locate information of interest.

RENAME A WORKSHEET

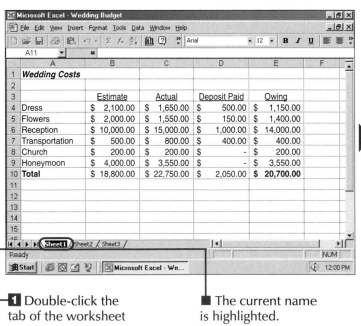

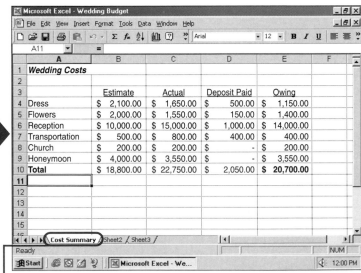

1 Double-click the tab of the worksheet you want to rename.

■ The current name is highlighted.

2 Type a new name and then press the **Enter** key.

Note: A worksheet name can contain up to 31 characters, including spaces.

154

MOVE A WORKSHEET

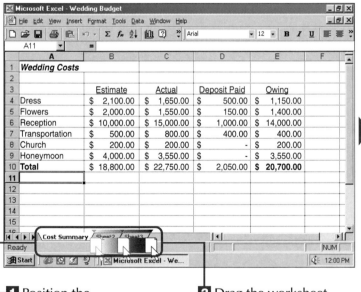

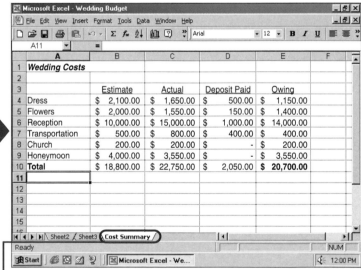

1 Position the mouse ⬐ over the tab of the worksheet you want to move.

2 Drag the worksheet to a new location.

■ An arrow (▼) shows where the worksheet will appear.

■ The worksheet appears in the new location.

MOVE OR COPY DATA BETWEEN WORKSHEETS

You can move or copy data from one worksheet to another. This will save you time when you want to use data from another worksheet.

MOVE OR COPY DATA BETWEEN WORKSHEETS

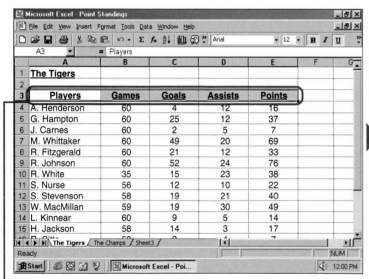

1 Select the cells containing the data you want to move or copy to another worksheet. To select cells, see page 12.

2 Click one of the following buttons.

✂ Move data

📋 Copy data

Note: If the button you want is not displayed, click » on the Standard toolbar to display all the buttons.

Note: The Clipboard toolbar may appear when you move or copy data. To use the Clipboard toolbar, see page 49.

156

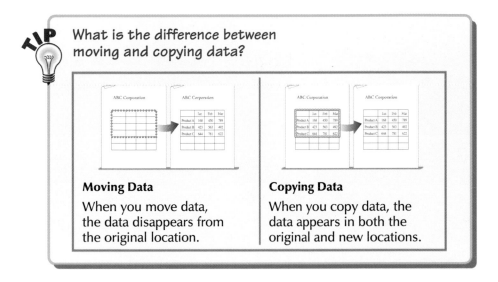

What is the difference between moving and copying data?

Moving Data

When you move data, the data disappears from the original location.

Copying Data

When you copy data, the data appears in both the original and new locations.

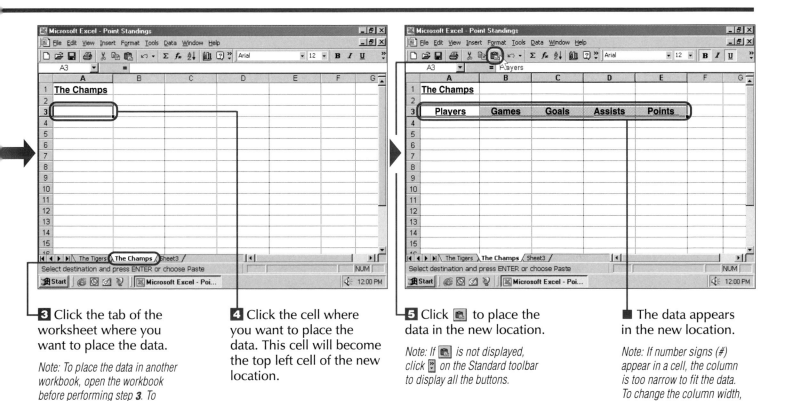

3 Click the tab of the worksheet where you want to place the data.

*Note: To place the data in another workbook, open the workbook before performing step **3**. To open a workbook, see page 34.*

4 Click the cell where you want to place the data. This cell will become the top left cell of the new location.

5 Click 🖺 to place the data in the new location.

Note: If 🖺 is not displayed, click 🔽 on the Standard toolbar to display all the buttons.

■ The data appears in the new location.

Note: If number signs (#) appear in a cell, the column is too narrow to fit the data. To change the column width, see page 98.

ENTER A FORMULA ACROSS WORKSHEETS

You can enter a formula in one worksheet that uses data from other worksheets.

ENTER A FORMULA ACROSS WORKSHEETS

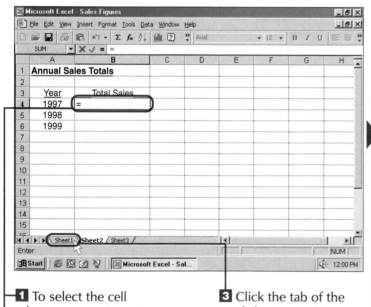

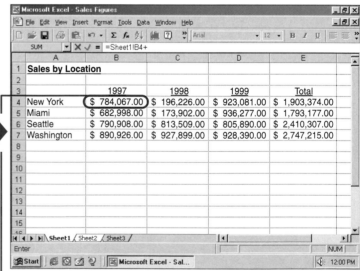

1 To select the cell where you want to enter a formula, click the cell.

2 Type an equal sign (=) to begin the formula.

3 Click the tab of the worksheet containing the data you want to use in the formula.

■ The worksheet appears.

4 Click a cell containing data you want to use in the formula.

5 Type the symbol for the calculation you want to perform, such as + or *.

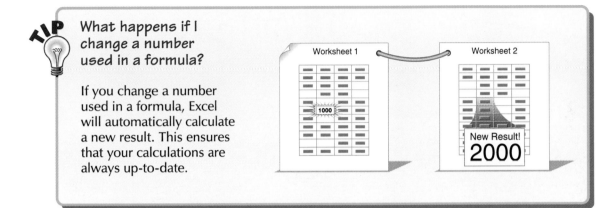

TIP

What happens if I change a number used in a formula?

If you change a number used in a formula, Excel will automatically calculate a new result. This ensures that your calculations are always up-to-date.

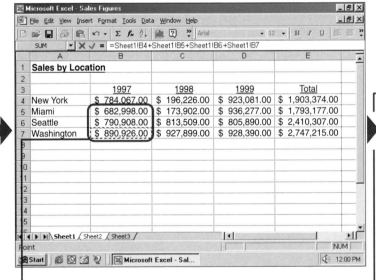

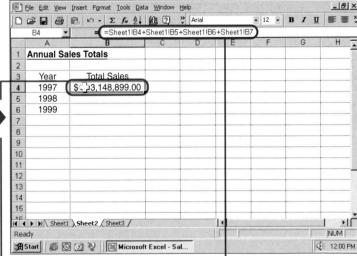

6 Repeat steps **3** to **5** until you have selected all the cells containing data you want to use in the formula.

*Note: In this example, cells **B4** to **B7** are added together.*

7 Press the Enter key to complete the formula.

■ The result of the calculation appears in the cell you selected in step **1**.

8 To view the formula you entered, click the cell containing the formula.

■ The formula bar displays the worksheet name and cell reference for each cell used in the formula.

CHAPTER 9

WORK WITH CHARTS

Are you interested in displaying your worksheet data in a chart? In this chapter you will learn how to create, change and print charts.

Introduction to Charts 162

Create a Chart 164

Move or Size a Chart 168

Print a Chart 170

Change Chart Type 172

Change Chart Titles 174

Change the Way Data is Plotted 175

Add Data to a Chart 176

INTRODUCTION TO CHARTS

A chart allows you to visually display your worksheet data. Excel offers many different chart types.

PARTS OF A CHART

Data Series

A group of related data representing one row or column from your worksheet. Each data series is represented by a specific color, pattern or symbol.

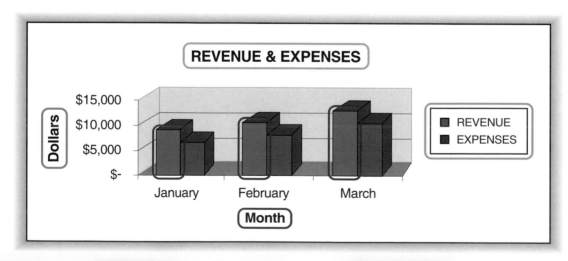

Chart Title

Identifies the subject of your chart.

Legend

Identifies the color, pattern or symbol that represents each data series in your chart.

Value Axis Title

Indicates the unit of measure used in your chart.

Category Axis Title

Indicates the categories used in your chart.

COMMON CHART TYPES

Area

An area chart is useful for showing the amount of change in data over time. Each line represents a data series.

Line

A line chart is useful for showing changes to data at regular intervals. Each line represents a data series.

Column

A column chart is useful for showing changes to data over time or comparing individual items. Each column represents an item in a data series.

Bar

A bar chart is useful for comparing individual items. Each bar represents an item in a data series.

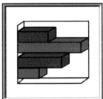

Pie

A pie chart is useful for showing the relationship of parts to a whole. Each piece of a pie represents an item in a data series. A pie chart can show only one data series at a time.

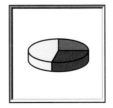

Doughnut

A doughnut chart is useful for showing the relationship of parts to a whole. Unlike a pie chart, a doughnut chart can display more than one data series. Each ring represents a data series.

Radar

A radar chart is useful for comparing the items in several data series. Each data series is shown as a line around a central point.

XY (Scatter)

An xy (scatter) chart is useful for showing the relationship between two or more data series measured at uneven intervals.

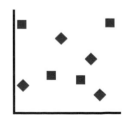

CREATE A CHART

You can create a chart to graphically display your worksheet data.

CREATE A CHART

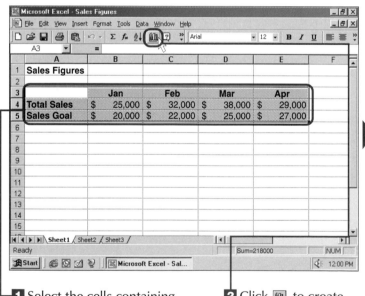

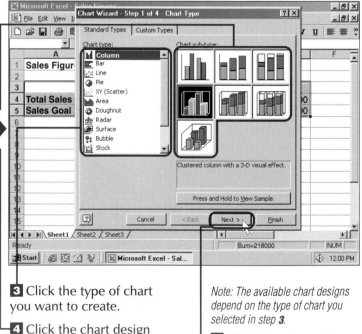

1 Select the cells containing the data you want to display in a chart, including the row and column labels. To select cells, see page 12.

2 Click 📊 to create the chart.

Note: If 📊 is not displayed, click ⏩ on the Standard toolbar to display all the buttons.

■ The Chart Wizard appears.

3 Click the type of chart you want to create.

4 Click the chart design you want to use.

*Note: The available chart designs depend on the type of chart you selected in step **3**.*

5 Click **Next** to continue.

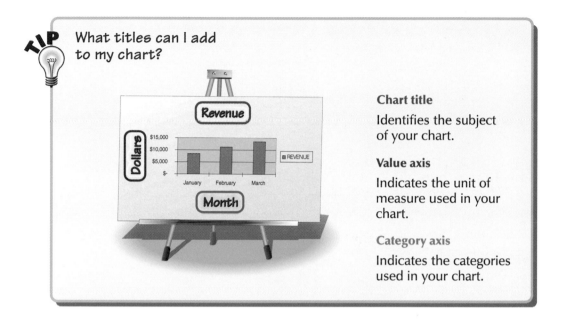

What titles can I add to my chart?

Chart title

Identifies the subject of your chart.

Value axis

Indicates the unit of measure used in your chart.

Category axis

Indicates the categories used in your chart.

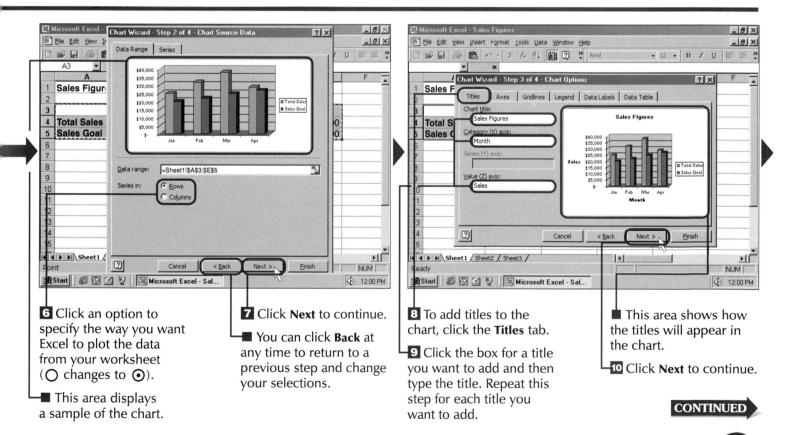

6 Click an option to specify the way you want Excel to plot the data from your worksheet (○ changes to ●).

■ This area displays a sample of the chart.

7 Click **Next** to continue.

■ You can click **Back** at any time to return to a previous step and change your selections.

8 To add titles to the chart, click the **Titles** tab.

9 Click the box for a title you want to add and then type the title. Repeat this step for each title you want to add.

■ This area shows how the titles will appear in the chart.

10 Click **Next** to continue.

CONTINUED

CREATE A CHART

When creating a chart, you can choose to display the chart on the same worksheet as the data or on its own sheet, called a chart sheet.

CREATE A CHART (CONTINUED)

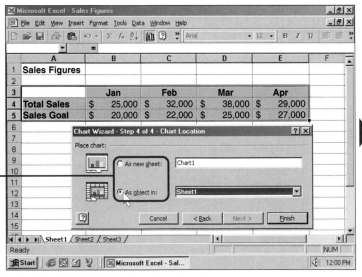

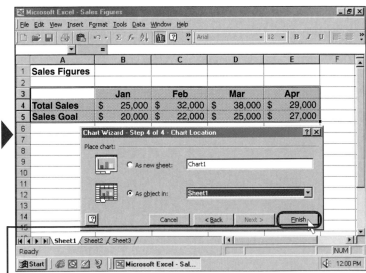

11 Click an option to specify where you want to display the chart (○ changes to ⊙).

As new sheet

Display chart on its own sheet, called a chart sheet

As object in

Display chart on the same worksheet as the data

12 Click **Finish** to complete the chart.

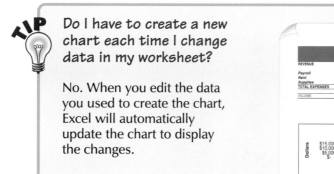

TIP

Do I have to create a new chart each time I change data in my worksheet?

No. When you edit the data you used to create the chart, Excel will automatically update the chart to display the changes.

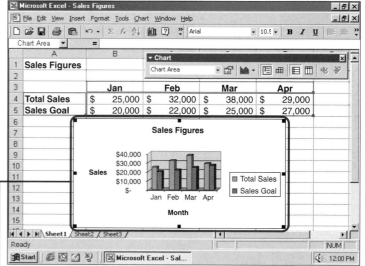

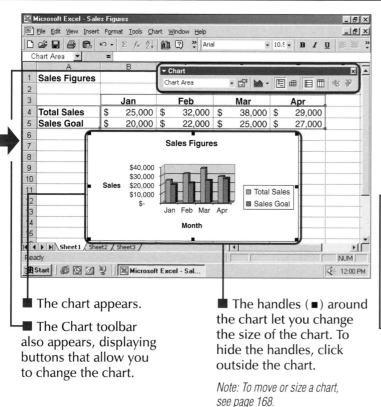

■ The chart appears.

■ The Chart toolbar also appears, displaying buttons that allow you to change the chart.

■ The handles (■) around the chart let you change the size of the chart. To hide the handles, click outside the chart.

Note: To move or size a chart, see page 168.

DELETE A CHART

1 Click a blank area in the chart. Handles (■) appear around the chart.

2 Press the `Delete` key.

Note: To delete a chart displayed on a chart sheet, you must delete the sheet. To delete a worksheet, see page 153.

MOVE OR SIZE A CHART

After you create a chart, you can change the location or size of the chart.

– Move –

– Size –

MOVE A CHART

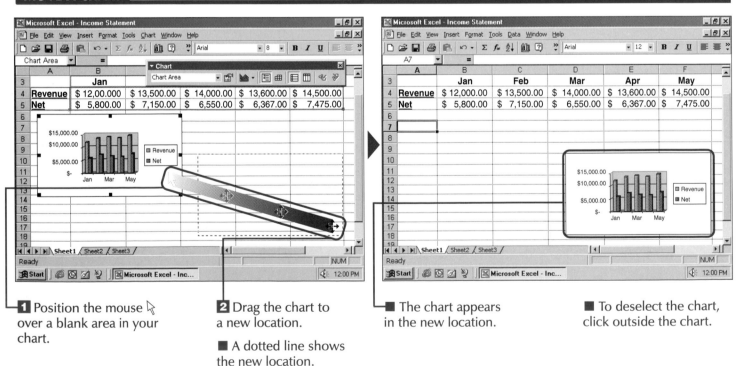

1 Position the mouse ⌖ over a blank area in your chart.

2 Drag the chart to a new location.

■ A dotted line shows the new location.

■ The chart appears in the new location.

■ To deselect the chart, click outside the chart.

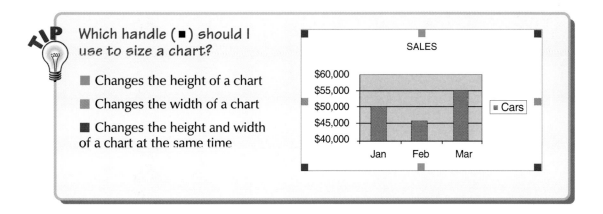

TIP

Which handle (■) should I use to size a chart?

■ Changes the height of a chart

■ Changes the width of a chart

■ Changes the height and width of a chart at the same time

SIZE A CHART

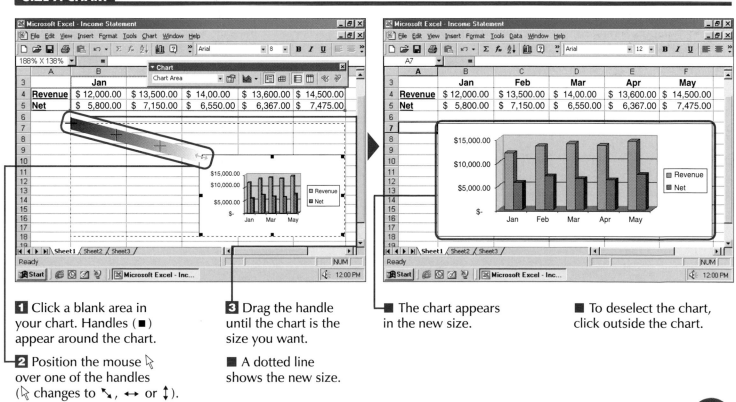

1 Click a blank area in your chart. Handles (■) appear around the chart.

2 Position the mouse ⍐ over one of the handles (⍐ changes to ⬉, ↔ or ↕).

3 Drag the handle until the chart is the size you want.

■ A dotted line shows the new size.

■ The chart appears in the new size.

■ To deselect the chart, click outside the chart.

PRINT A CHART

You can print your chart with the worksheet data or on its own page.

Print a chart with worksheet data

Print a chart on its own page

PRINT A CHART WITH WORKSHEET DATA

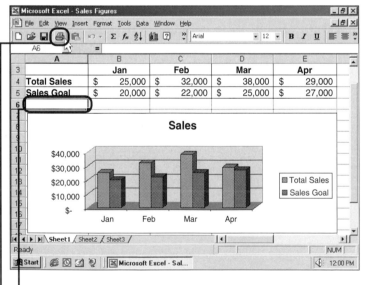

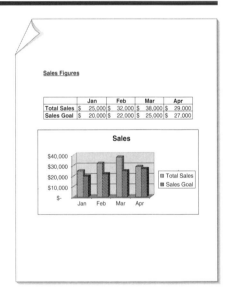

1 Click a cell outside the chart.

2 Click 🖨 to print the chart with your worksheet data.

Note: If 🖨 is not displayed, click ⏩ on the Standard toolbar to display all the buttons.

■ The chart prints with the worksheet data.

TIP

Can I see how my chart will look when printed?

You can preview your chart to see how the chart will look when printed. This lets you confirm that the chart will print the way you want. For information on using the Print Preview feature, see page 128.

PRINT A CHART ON ITS OWN PAGE

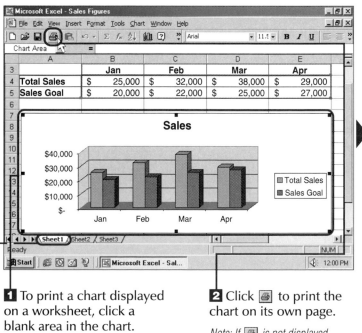

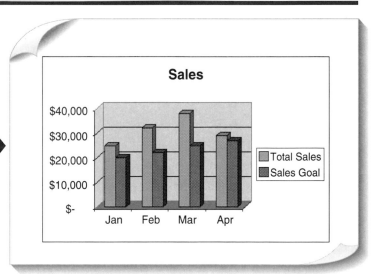

1 To print a chart displayed on a worksheet, click a blank area in the chart.

■ To print a chart displayed on a chart sheet, click the tab for the chart sheet.

2 Click 🖨 to print the chart on its own page.

Note: If 🖨 is not displayed, click ➤ on the Standard toolbar to display all the buttons.

■ When you print a chart on its own page, the chart expands to fill the page. The printed chart may look different from the chart on your screen.

After you create a chart, you can select a different type of chart that will better suit your data.

CHANGE CHART TYPE

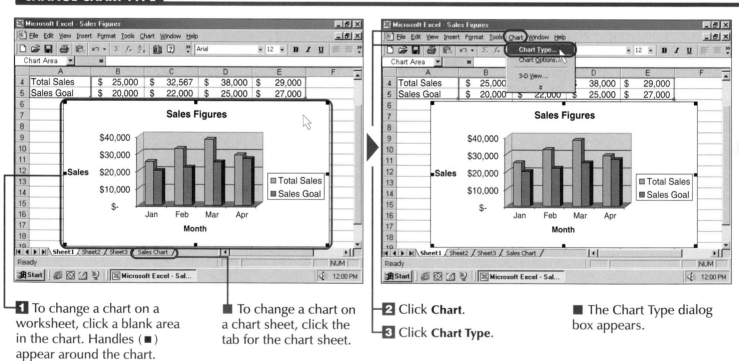

1 To change a chart on a worksheet, click a blank area in the chart. Handles (■) appear around the chart.

■ To change a chart on a chart sheet, click the tab for the chart sheet.

2 Click **Chart**.

3 Click **Chart Type**.

■ The Chart Type dialog box appears.

TIP

What type of chart should I choose?

The type of chart you should choose depends on your data. Each chart type presents data in a specific way. For example, area, column and line charts are ideal for showing changes to values over time. Pie charts are ideal for showing percentages.

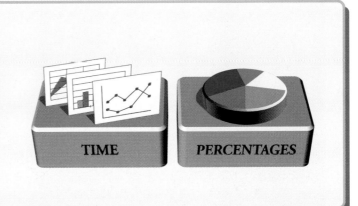

TIME   PERCENTAGES

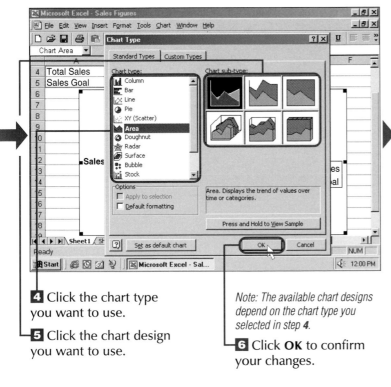

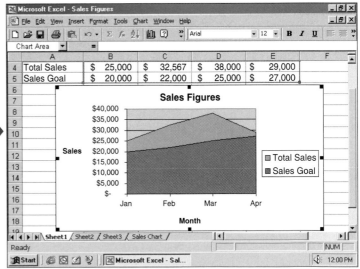

4 Click the chart type you want to use.

5 Click the chart design you want to use.

Note: The available chart designs depend on the chart type you selected in step 4.

6 Click **OK** to confirm your changes.

■ The chart displays the chart type you selected.

CHANGE CHART TITLES

You can change the titles in your chart to make the titles more meaningful.

CHANGE CHART TITLES

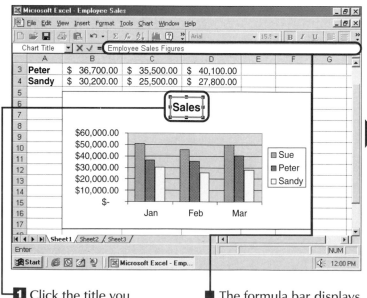

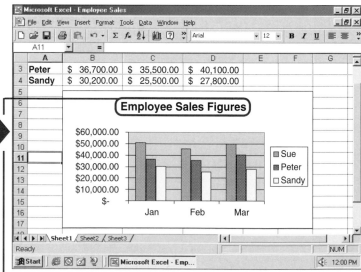

1 Click the title you want to change. A border appears around the title.

2 Type the new title.

■ The formula bar displays the title as you type.

3 Press the Enter key to add the title to the chart.

■ The chart displays the new title.

■ To deselect the title, click outside the chart.

CHANGE THE WAY DATA IS PLOTTED

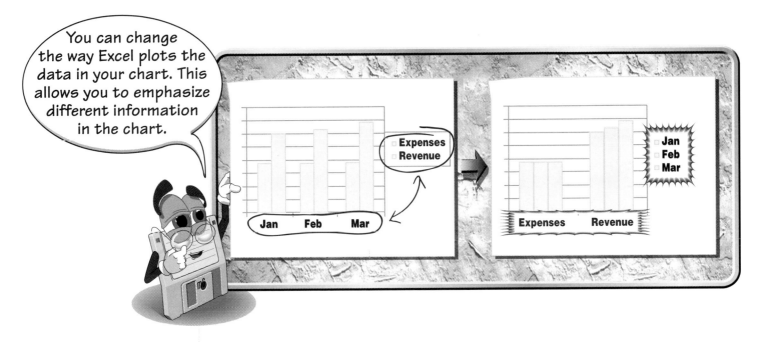

You can change the way Excel plots the data in your chart. This allows you to emphasize different information in the chart.

CHANGE THE WAY DATA IS PLOTTED

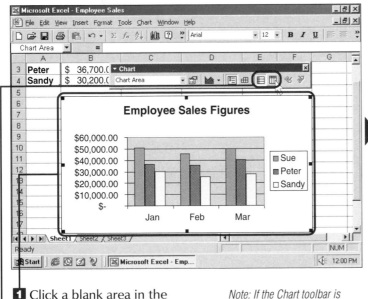

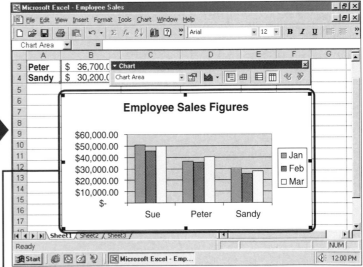

1 Click a blank area in the chart you want to change.

2 Click one of the following buttons.

▤ Plot data by row

▥ Plot data by column

Note: If the Chart toolbar is not displayed, see page 21 to display the toolbar.

■ The chart displays the change.

ADD DATA TO A CHART

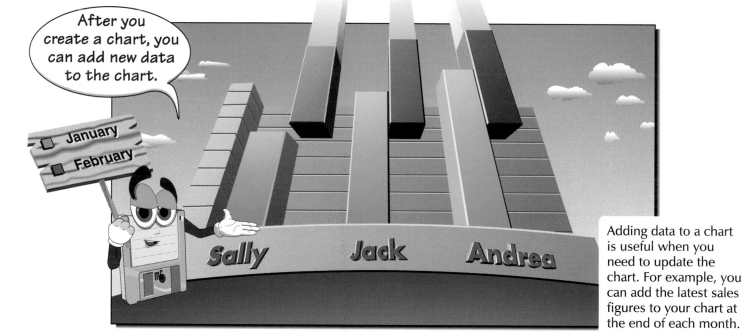

After you create a chart, you can add new data to the chart.

Adding data to a chart is useful when you need to update the chart. For example, you can add the latest sales figures to your chart at the end of each month.

ADD DATA TO A CHART

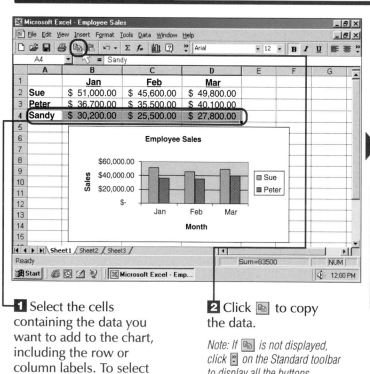

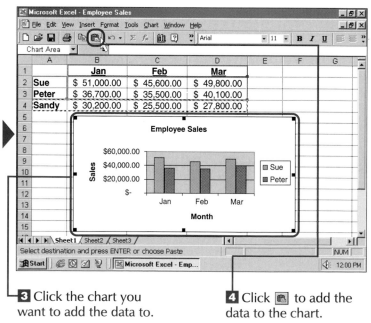

1 Select the cells containing the data you want to add to the chart, including the row or column labels. To select cells, see page 12.

2 Click 📋 to copy the data.

Note: If 📋 is not displayed, click ⟫ on the Standard toolbar to display all the buttons.

3 Click the chart you want to add the data to.

4 Click 📋 to add the data to the chart.

Note: If 📋 is not displayed, click ⟫ on the Standard toolbar to display all the buttons.

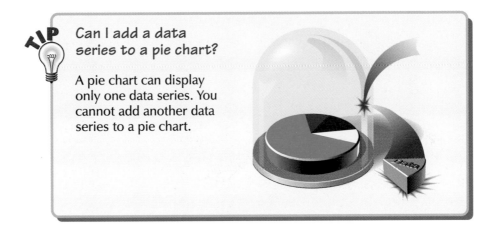

Can I add a data series to a pie chart?

A pie chart can display only one data series. You cannot add another data series to a pie chart.

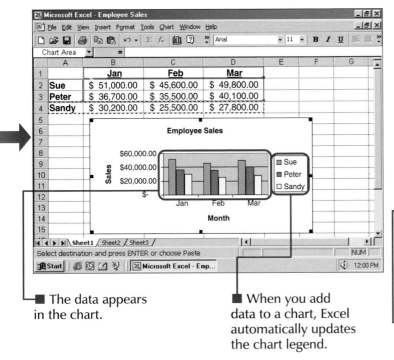

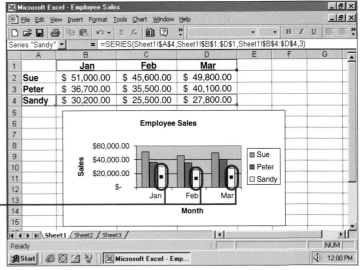

■ The data appears in the chart.

■ When you add data to a chart, Excel automatically updates the chart legend.

DELETE DATA FROM A CHART

1 Click the data you want to remove from the chart. Handles (■) appear on the data series.

2 Press the Delete key to delete the data from the chart.

CHAPTER 10

WORK WITH GRAPHICS

Are you wondering how to use graphics to enhance the appearance of your worksheet? This chapter shows you how.

Add an AutoShape 180

Add a Text Effect 182

Add a Text Box 184

Move or Size a Graphic 186

Change Color of a Graphic 188

Make a Graphic 3-D 189

Excel provides many ready-made shapes, called AutoShapes, that you can add to your worksheet or chart.

AutoShapes can help illustrate information or draw attention to important data in your worksheet.

ADD AN AUTOSHAPE

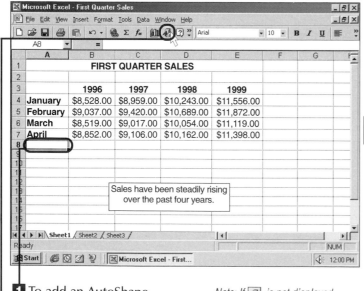

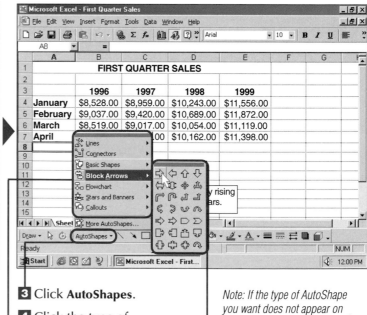

1 To add an AutoShape to your worksheet, click a cell in the worksheet.

■ To add an AutoShape to a chart, click the chart.

2 Click 🖼 to display the Drawing toolbar.

Note: If 🖼 is not displayed, click 🔽 on the Standard toolbar to display all the buttons.

■ The Drawing toolbar appears.

3 Click **AutoShapes**.

4 Click the type of AutoShape you want to add.

Note: If the type of AutoShape you want does not appear on the menu, position the mouse ⌀ over the bottom of the menu to display all the menu commands.

5 Click the AutoShape you want to add.

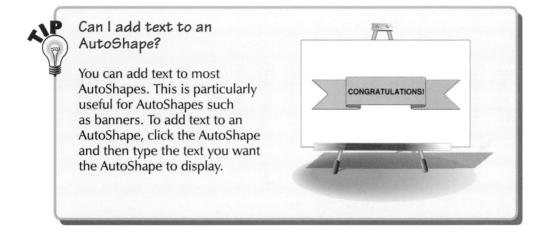

TIP

Can I add text to an
AutoShape?

You can add text to most
AutoShapes. This is particularly
useful for AutoShapes such
as banners. To add text to an
AutoShape, click the AutoShape
and then type the text you want
the AutoShape to display.

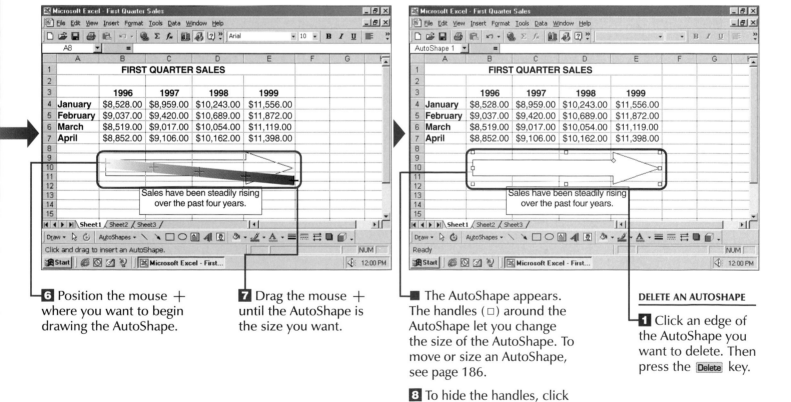

6 Position the mouse +
where you want to begin
drawing the AutoShape.

7 Drag the mouse +
until the AutoShape is
the size you want.

■ The AutoShape appears.
The handles (□) around the
AutoShape let you change
the size of the AutoShape. To
move or size an AutoShape,
see page 186.

8 To hide the handles, click
outside the AutoShape.

*Note: To hide the Drawing toolbar,
repeat step 2.*

DELETE AN AUTOSHAPE

1 Click an edge of
the AutoShape you
want to delete. Then
press the Delete key.

You can use the WordArt feature to add a text effect to your worksheet or chart.

Adding a text effect is an easy way to create an eye-catching title or heading.

ADD A TEXT EFFECT

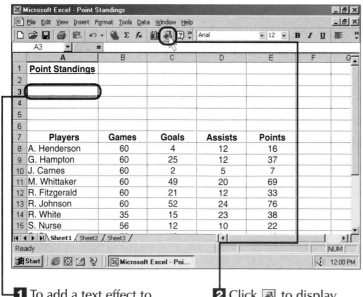

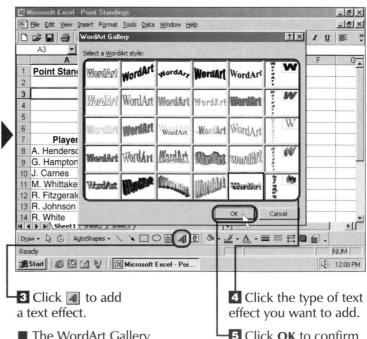

1 To add a text effect to your worksheet, click a cell in the worksheet.

■ To add a text effect to a chart, click the chart.

2 Click 🖉 to display the Drawing toolbar.

Note: If 🖉 is not displayed, click 🔛 on the Standard toolbar to display all the buttons.

■ The Drawing toolbar appears.

3 Click 🔳 to add a text effect.

■ The WordArt Gallery dialog box appears.

4 Click the type of text effect you want to add.

5 Click **OK** to confirm your selection.

TIP

How do I edit a text effect?

Double-click the text effect to display the Edit WordArt Text dialog box. Then edit the text in the dialog box. When you finish editing the text effect, click **OK**.

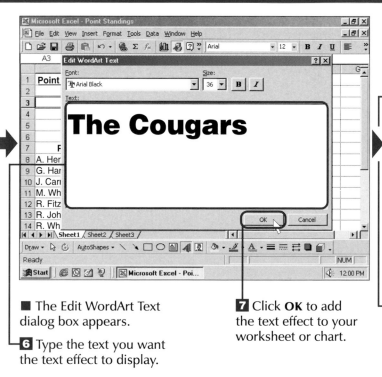

■ The Edit WordArt Text dialog box appears.

6 Type the text you want the text effect to display.

7 Click **OK** to add the text effect to your worksheet or chart.

■ The text effect appears. The handles (□) around the text effect let you change the size of the text effect. To move or size a text effect, see page 186.

8 To hide the handles, click outside the text effect.

Note: To hide the Drawing toolbar, repeat step 2.

DELETE A TEXT EFFECT

1 Click the text effect you want to delete. Then press the **Delete** key.

ADD A TEXT BOX

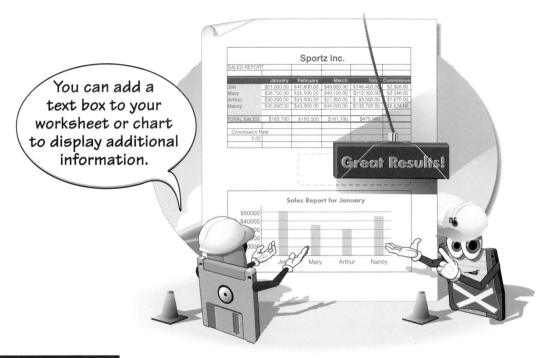

You can add a text box to your worksheet or chart to display additional information.

Text boxes are useful for displaying notes. You can also use text boxes to label or describe items in your worksheet or chart.

ADD A TEXT BOX

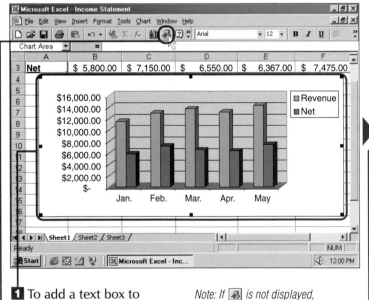

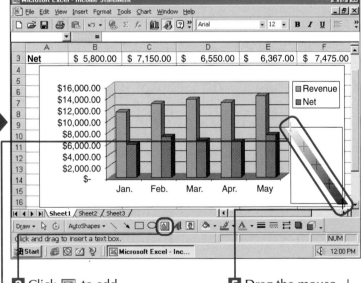

1 To add a text box to a chart, click the chart.

■ To add a text box to your worksheet, click a cell in the worksheet.

2 Click 🖉 to display the Drawing toolbar.

Note: If 🖉 is not displayed, click 🔽 on the Standard toolbar to display all the buttons.

■ The Drawing toolbar appears.

3 Click 🖾 to add a text box.

4 Position the mouse ‡ where you want to begin drawing the text box.

5 Drag the mouse + until the text box is the size you want.

How do I edit the text in a text box?

To edit the text, click the text box and then edit the text as you would edit any text in your worksheet. When you finish editing the text, click outside the text box.

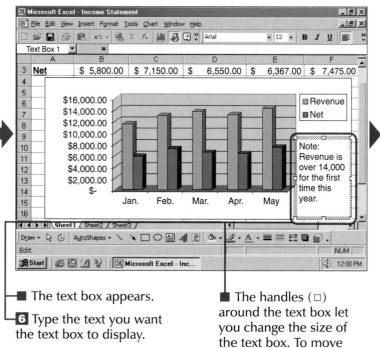

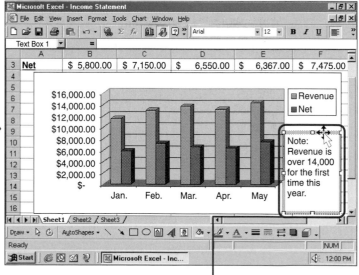

■ The text box appears.

6 Type the text you want the text box to display.

■ The handles (□) around the text box let you change the size of the text box. To move or size a text box, see page 186.

7 To hide the handles, click outside the text box.

Note: To hide the Drawing toolbar, repeat step 2.

DELETE A TEXT BOX

1 Click the text box you want to delete.

2 Click an edge of the text box and then press the Delete key.

MOVE OR SIZE A GRAPHIC

You can change the location or size of a graphic in your worksheet.

- MOVE -

- SIZE -

MOVE A GRAPHIC

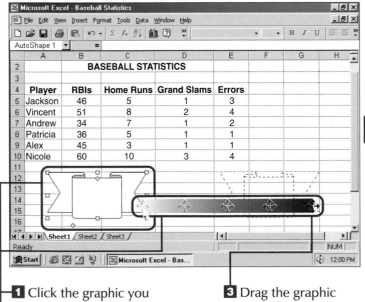

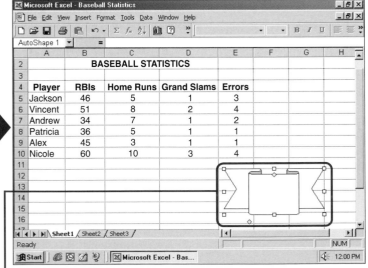

1 Click the graphic you want to move. Handles (□) appear around the graphic.

2 Position the mouse ⊕ over an edge of the graphic you want to move (⊕ changes to ✥).

3 Drag the graphic to a new location.

■ The graphic appears in the new location.

Note: If you added a graphic to a chart, you cannot move the graphic outside the chart area.

186

TIP

Which handle (□) should I use to size a graphic?

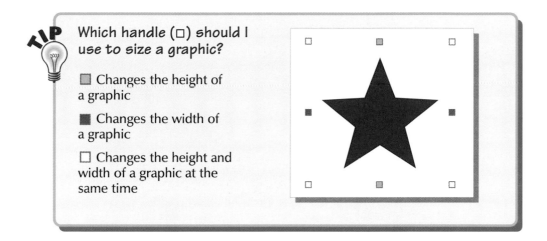

■ Changes the height of a graphic

■ Changes the width of a graphic

□ Changes the height and width of a graphic at the same time

SIZE A GRAPHIC

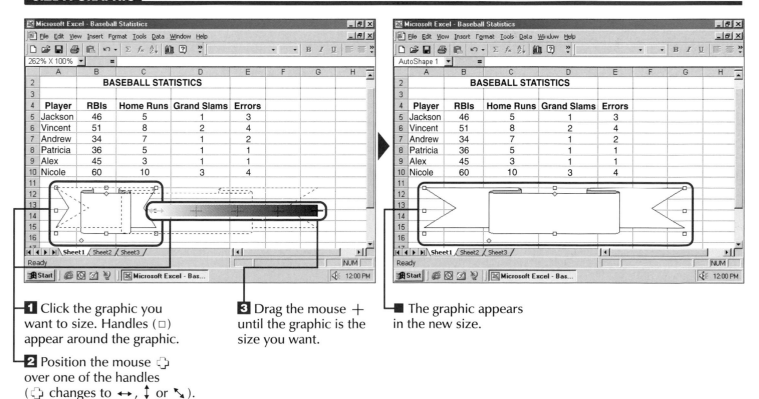

1 Click the graphic you want to size. Handles (□) appear around the graphic.

2 Position the mouse ⟐ over one of the handles (⟐ changes to ↔, ↕ or ↘).

3 Drag the mouse + until the graphic is the size you want.

■ The graphic appears in the new size.

CHANGE COLOR OF A GRAPHIC

You can change the color of a graphic in your worksheet or chart.

CHANGE COLOR OF A GRAPHIC

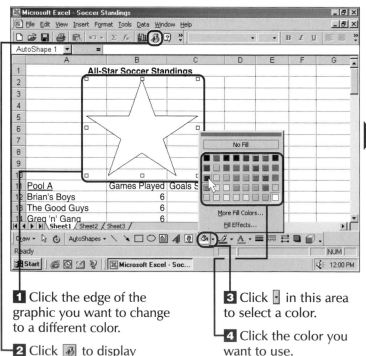

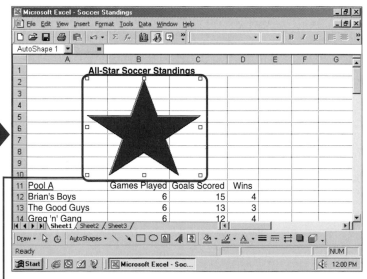

1 Click the edge of the graphic you want to change to a different color.

2 Click 🎨 to display the Drawing toolbar.

Note: If 🎨 is not displayed, click 🔽 on the Standard toolbar to display all the buttons.

3 Click ⏷ in this area to select a color.

4 Click the color you want to use.

■ The graphic displays the new color.

Note: To hide the Drawing toolbar, repeat step 2.

■ To remove the color from a graphic, repeat steps **1** to **4**, except select **No Fill** in step **4**.

188

MAKE A GRAPHIC 3-D

You can make a graphic in your worksheet or chart appear three-dimensional.

MAKE A GRAPHIC 3-D

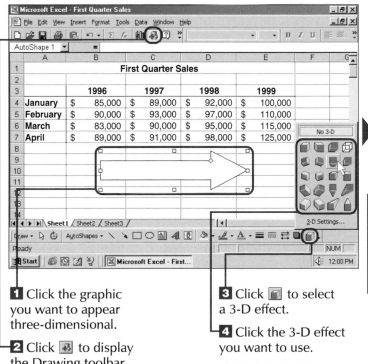

1 Click the graphic you want to appear three-dimensional.

2 Click ![icon] to display the Drawing toolbar.

Note: If ![icon] is not displayed, click ![icon] on the Standard toolbar to display all the buttons.

3 Click ![icon] to select a 3-D effect.

4 Click the 3-D effect you want to use.

Note: If the 3-D effects are dimmed, you cannot make the graphic you selected three-dimensional.

■ The graphic displays the 3-D effect.

Note: To hide the Drawing toolbar, repeat step 2.

■ To remove a 3-D effect from a graphic, repeat steps **1** to **4**, except select **No 3-D** in step **4**.

LAST NAME	FIRST NAME	PRODUCT	UNITS SO
Marcuson	Jason	A	63
Mathews	Kathleen	A	162
Petterson	Brenda	A	68
Robinson	Melanie	A	81
Smith	Jill	B	95
Smith	Linda	B	70
ns	Allen	B	59
		B Subtotal	225
	huck	C	93
	Jim	C	79
		C Subtotal	172
A Subtotal			3754

CHAPTER 11

MANAGE DATA IN A LIST

Would you like Excel to help you organize a large collection of data? In this chapter you will learn how to sort data in a list, add subtotals to a list and more.

Create a List .192

Sort Data in a List 194

Filter a List .198

Add Subtotals to a List 202

You can create a list to organize a large collection of data.

Common lists include mailing lists, phone directories, product lists, library book catalogs, music collections and wine lists.

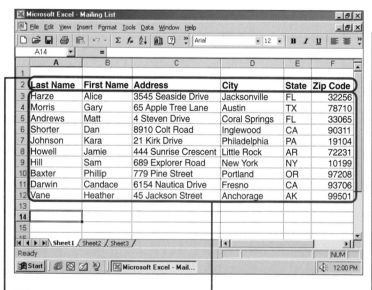

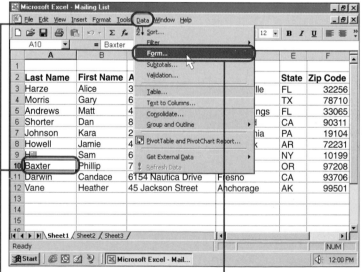

1 Type the column labels that describe the data you will enter into each column.

Note: You should bold the column labels to ensure that Excel will recognize the text as column labels. To bold text, see page 102.

2 Type the information for each record. Do not leave any blank rows in the list.

Note: You can edit data in the list as you would in any worksheet.

ADD RECORDS USING A DATA FORM

1 Click a cell in the list.

2 Click **Data**.

3 Click **Form**.

Note: If Form does not appear on the menu, position the mouse over the bottom of the menu to display all the menu commands.

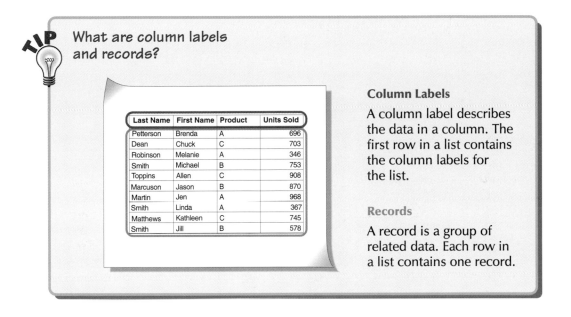

TIP

What are column labels and records?

Last Name	First Name	Product	Units Sold
Petterson	Brenda	A	696
Dean	Chuck	C	703
Robinson	Melanie	A	346
Smith	Michael	B	753
Toppins	Allen	C	908
Marcuson	Jason	B	870
Martin	Jen	A	968
Smith	Linda	A	367
Matthews	Kathleen	C	745
Smith	Jill	B	578

Column Labels

A column label describes the data in a column. The first row in a list contains the column labels for the list.

Records

A record is a group of related data. Each row in a list contains one record.

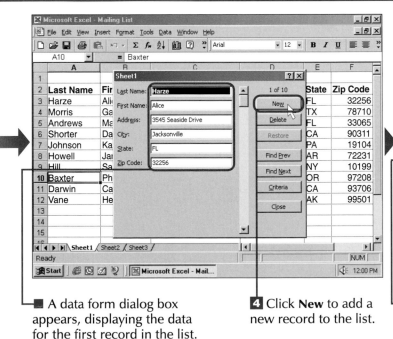

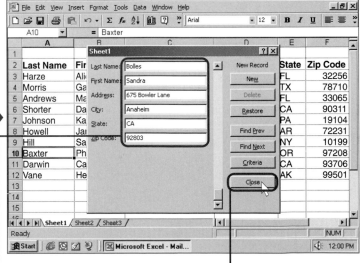

■ A data form dialog box appears, displaying the data for the first record in the list.

4 Click **New** to add a new record to the list.

5 Type the data that corresponds to the first column label and then press the **Tab** key. Repeat this step until you have entered all the information for the record.

6 Repeat steps **4** and **5** for each record you want to add.

7 Click **Close** when you have finished entering records.

SORT DATA IN A LIST

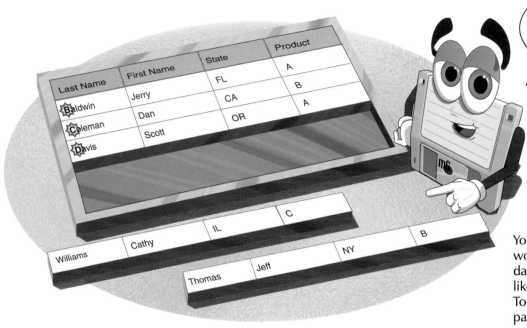

You can organize your list by changing the order of the data.

You should save your workbook before sorting data in case you do not like the results of the sort. To save a workbook, see page 28.

SORT BY ONE COLUMN

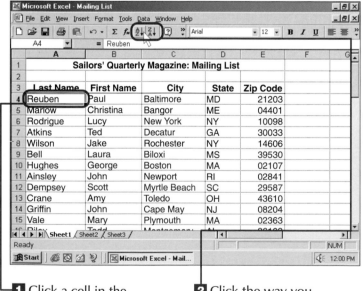

1 Click a cell in the column you want to sort by.

2 Click the way you want to sort the data.

⬇ Sort 0 to 9, A to Z

⬆ Sort 9 to 0, Z to A

Note: If the button you want is not displayed, click ⸬ on the Standard toolbar to display all the buttons.

■ The data in the list appears in the new order.

■ In this example, the data is sorted by last name.

Why would I sort my data by more than one column?

Sorting by more than one column allows you to further organize the data in your list. For example, if a last name appears more than once in the last name column, you can sort by a second column, such as the first name column.

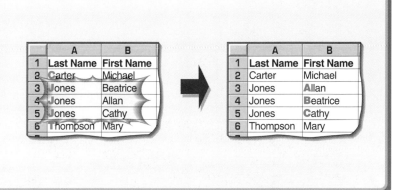

SORT BY TWO COLUMNS

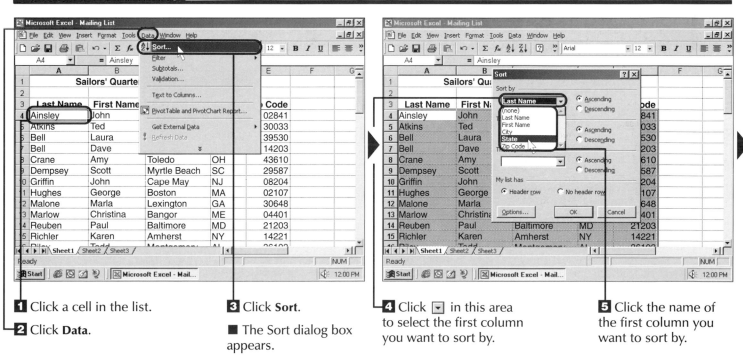

1 Click a cell in the list.

2 Click **Data**.

3 Click **Sort**.

■ The Sort dialog box appears.

4 Click ▾ in this area to select the first column you want to sort by.

5 Click the name of the first column you want to sort by.

CONTINUED

SORT DATA IN A LIST

You can sort the data in your list by letter, number or date.

LETTER	NUMBER	DATE
A	100	Jan-99
B	200	Feb-99
C	300	Mar-99
D	400	Apr-99
E	500	May-99
F	600	Jun-99
G	700	Jul-99
H	800	Aug-99

SORT BY TWO COLUMNS (CONTINUED)

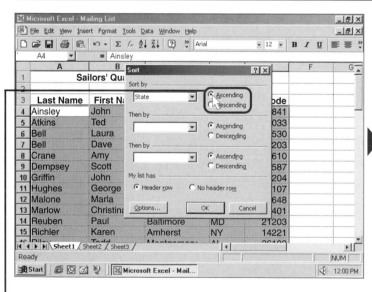

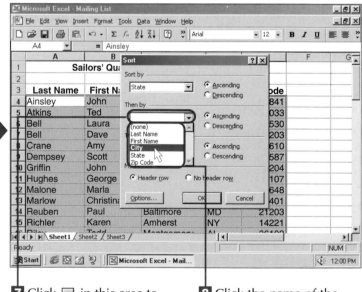

6 Click the way you want to sort the first column (○ changes to ⊙).

Ascending

Sort 0 to 9, A to Z

Descending

Sort 9 to 0, Z to A

7 Click ▼ in this area to select the second column you want to sort by.

8 Click the name of the column you want to sort by.

**How often can I sort
the data in my list?**

You can sort the data in
your list as often as you
like. Sorting is useful if
you frequently add new
data to your list.

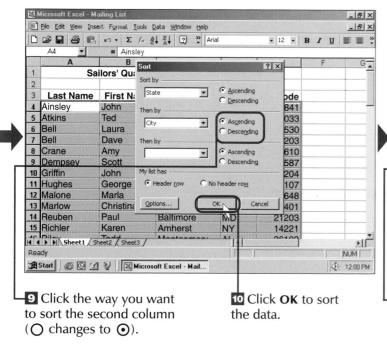

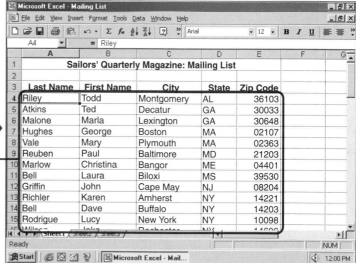

█▄**9** Click the way you want
to sort the second column
(○ changes to ⊙).

10 Click **OK** to sort
the data.

■ The data in the list
appears in the new order.

■ In this example, the
data is sorted by state.
When a state appears
more than once in the
list, the data is then
sorted by city.

You can filter your list to display only the records containing the data you want to review.

The AutoFilter feature allows you to analyze your data by placing related records together and hiding the records you do not want to review.

FILTER A LIST

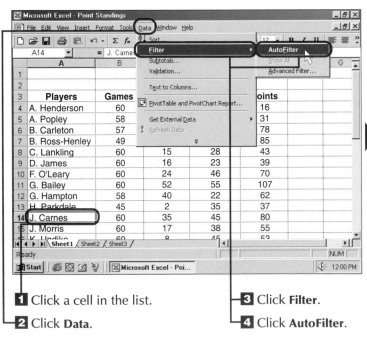

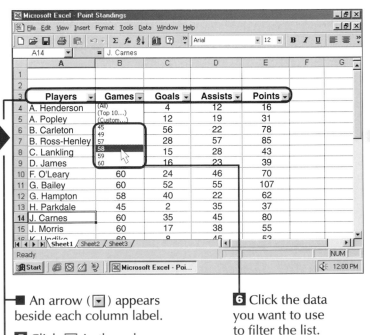

1 Click a cell in the list.

2 Click **Data**.

3 Click **Filter**.

4 Click **AutoFilter**.

■ An arrow (▾) appears beside each column label.

5 Click ▾ in the column containing the data you want to use to filter the list.

6 Click the data you want to use to filter the list.

TIP

How do I turn off the
AutoFilter feature when
I no longer want to filter
my list?

To turn off the AutoFilter
feature, repeat steps **2** to **4**
on page 198.

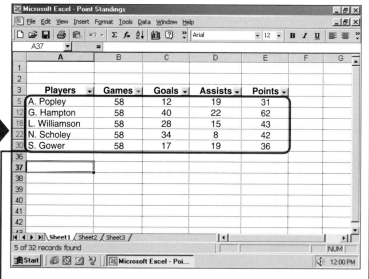

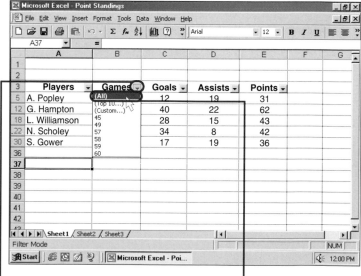

■ The list displays only
the records containing
the data you specified.
The other records are
temporarily hidden.

■ In this example, the
list displays only the
records for players who
have played 58 games.

REDISPLAY ALL RECORDS

1 To once again display
all the records, click ▾
in the column containing
the data you used to
filter the list.

2 Click (**All**).

199

FILTER A LIST

You can filter your list to display only records containing data within a specific range.

For example, you can display records for employees whose sales are greater than or equal to $500.

FILTER A LIST BY COMPARING DATA

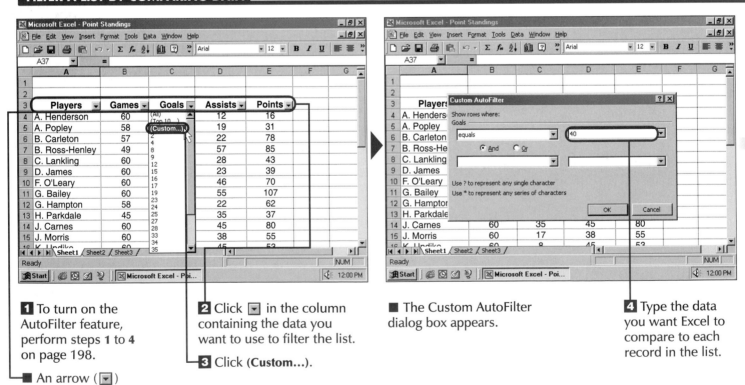

1 To turn on the AutoFilter feature, perform steps **1** to **4** on page 198.

■ An arrow (🔽) appears beside each column label.

2 Click 🔽 in the column containing the data you want to use to filter the list.

3 Click (**Custom...**).

■ The Custom AutoFilter dialog box appears.

4 Type the data you want Excel to compare to each record in the list.

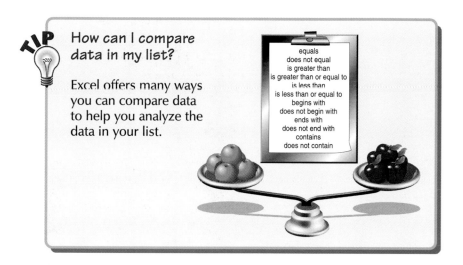

How can I compare data in my list?

Excel offers many ways you can compare data to help you analyze the data in your list.

equals
does not equal
is greater than
is greater than or equal to
is less than
is less than or equal to
begins with
does not begin with
ends with
does not end with
contains
does not contain

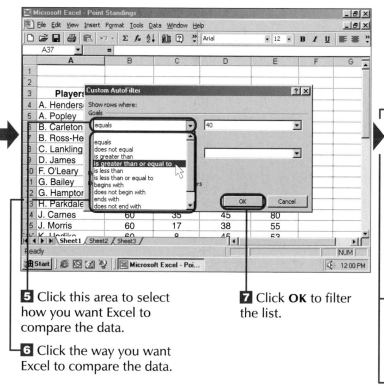

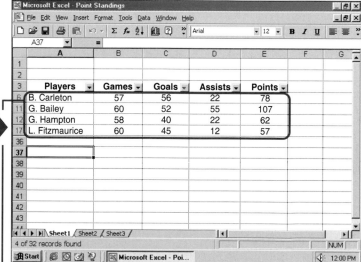

5 Click this area to select how you want Excel to compare the data.

6 Click the way you want Excel to compare the data.

7 Click **OK** to filter the list.

■ The list displays only the records containing the data you specified. The other records are temporarily hidden.

■ In this example, the list displays only the records for players who have scored 40 goals or more.

■ To once again display all the records, perform steps **1** and **2** on page 199.

■ To turn off the AutoFilter feature, perform steps **2** to **4** on page 198.

ADD SUBTOTALS TO A LIST

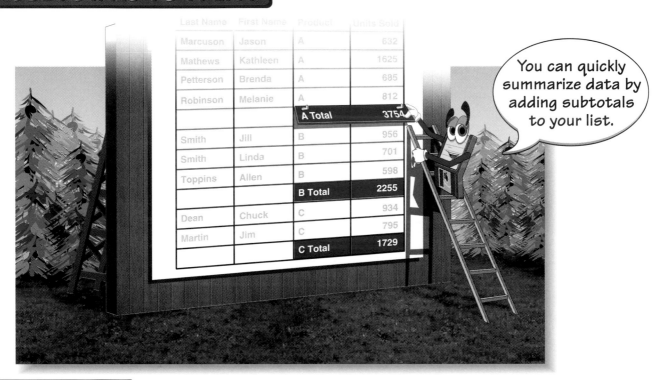

You can quickly summarize data by adding subtotals to your list.

ADD SUBTOTALS TO A LIST

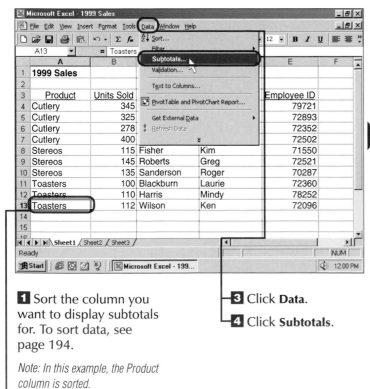

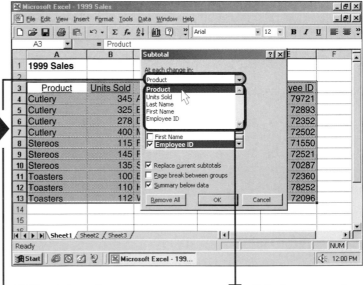

1 Sort the column you want to display subtotals for. To sort data, see page 194.

Note: In this example, the Product column is sorted.

2 Click a cell in the list.

3 Click **Data**.

4 Click **Subtotals**.

■ The Subtotal dialog box appears.

5 Click this area to select the column you want to display subtotals for.

6 Click the name of the column you want to display subtotals for.

Note: The column you select should be the same column you sorted in step 1.

How can subtotals help me?

You can use subtotals to help you analyze the data in your list and create a report for the data. For example, in a list containing department names and sales figures, you can use subtotals to find the total sales for each department and the grand total of all the sales.

QUARTERLY REPORT

Department	Salesperson	Sales
Automotive	L. Smith	$5,900
Automotive	M. Johnson	$8,500
Automotive	L. Hearn	$5,500
Automotive Total		**$19,900**
Housewares	C. Dean	$10,850
Housewares	G. Church	$4,000
Housewares	J. Smith	$5,000
Housewares Total		**$19,850**
Sports	J. Martin	$8,800
Sports	K. Gan	$10,000
Sports	J. Gledhill	$5,500
Sports Total		**$24,300**
Grand Total		**$64,050**

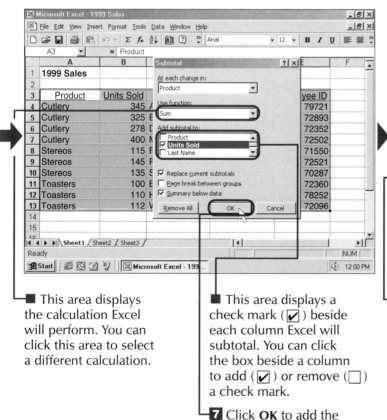

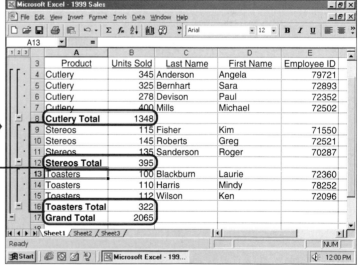

■ This area displays the calculation Excel will perform. You can click this area to select a different calculation.

■ This area displays a check mark (☑) beside each column Excel will subtotal. You can click the box beside a column to add (☑) or remove (☐) a check mark.

7 Click **OK** to add the subtotals to the list.

■ The list displays the subtotals and a grand total.

After adding subtotals to your list, you can display just the grand total, the subtotals or all the data in the list.

GRAND TOTAL

Last Name	First Name	Product	Units Sold
		Grand Total	8316

SUBTOTALS

Last Name	First Name	Product	Units Sold
		A Total	3754
		B Total	2255
		C Total	2307
		Grand Total	8316

ALL THE DATA

Last Name	First Name	Product	Units Sold
Marcuson	Jason	A	632
Matthews	Kathleen	A	1625
Petterson	Brenda	A	685
Robinson	Melanie	A	812
		A Total	3754
Smith	Jill	B	956
Smith	Linda	B	701
Toppins	Allen	B	598
		B Total	2255
Dean	Chuck	C	934
Martin	Jim	C	795
Smith	Michael	C	578
		C Total	2307
		Grand Total	8316

HIDE OR DISPLAY SUBTOTALED DATA

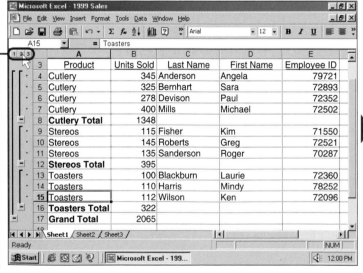

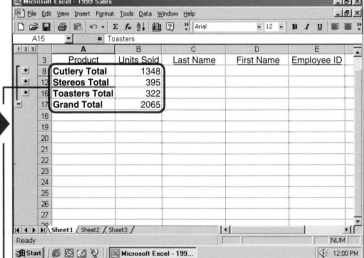

1 Click one of the following buttons.

1 Display only grand total

2 Display subtotals and grand total

3 Display all the data

■ Excel displays the data you specified. The other data is temporarily hidden.

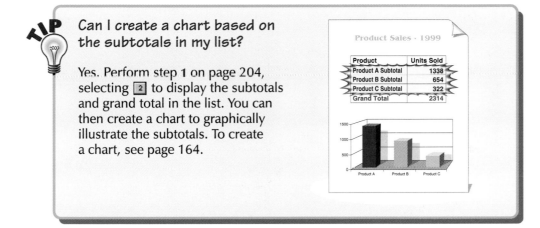

TIP

Can I create a chart based on the subtotals in my list?

Yes. Perform step 1 on page 204, selecting 2 to display the subtotals and grand total in the list. You can then create a chart to graphically illustrate the subtotals. To create a chart, see page 164.

Product Sales - 1999

Product	Units Sold
Product A Subtotal	1338
Product B Subtotal	654
Product C Subtotal	322
Grand Total	2314

REMOVE SUBTOTALS

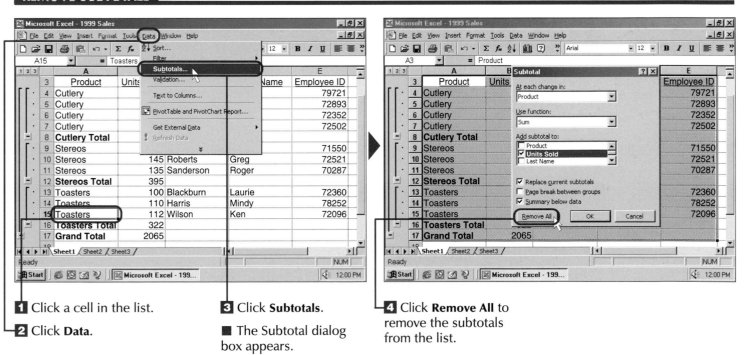

1 Click a cell in the list.

2 Click **Data**.

3 Click **Subtotals**.

■ The Subtotal dialog box appears.

4 Click **Remove All** to remove the subtotals from the list.

CHAPTER 12

EXCEL AND THE INTERNET

Are you wondering how you can use Excel to share data with other people on the Internet? In this chapter you will learn how to e-mail a worksheet, save a workbook as a Web page and more.

E-mail a Worksheet 208

Create a Hyperlink 210

Preview a Workbook as a Web Page . . .214

Save a Workbook as a Web Page 216

E-MAIL A WORKSHEET

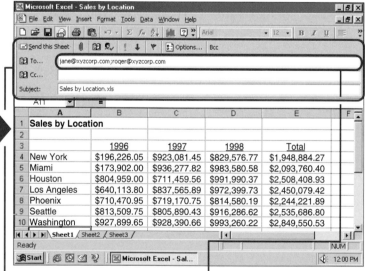

You can e-mail the worksheet displayed on your screen to a friend, family member or colleague.

Before you can e-mail a worksheet, Microsoft Outlook must be set up on your computer. Microsoft Outlook is a program that allows you to send and receive e-mail messages.

E-MAIL A WORKSHEET

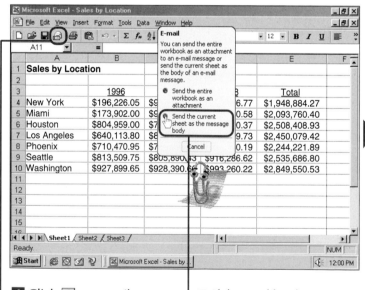

1 Click 🖳 to e-mail the current worksheet.

Note: If 🖳 is not displayed, click ☳ on the Standard toolbar to display all the buttons.

■ If the workbook contains data in more than one worksheet, a message appears, asking if you want to send the entire workbook or just the current worksheet.

2 Click this option to send the current worksheet.

■ An area appears for you to address the message.

3 Click this area and type the e-mail address of each person you want to receive the message. Separate each address with a semicolon (;).

**How do I e-mail an entire
workbook?**

To e-mail an entire workbook,
perform steps 1 to 5 below,
except select **Send the entire
workbook as an attachment** in
step 2. Then click **Send** to
send the message.

When you e-mail an entire
workbook, the workbook
appears as an icon in the
message.

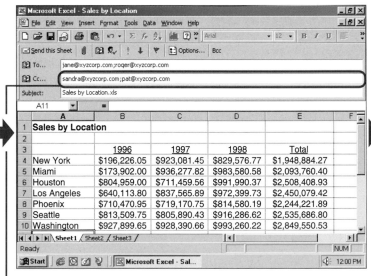

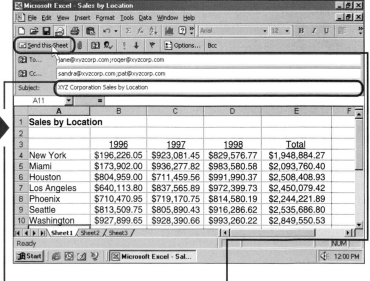

4 To send a copy of the
message, click this area and
type the e-mail address of
each person you want to
receive a copy. Separate
each address with a
semicolon (;).

*Note: You may want to send
a copy of the message to
people who are not directly
involved but would be
interested in the message.*

5 Click this area and
type a subject for the
message.

*Note: If a subject already exists,
you can drag the mouse I
over the existing subject and
then type a new subject.*

6 Click **Send this Sheet**
to send the message.

CREATE A HYPERLINK

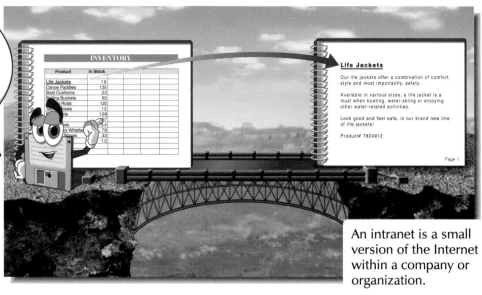

You can create a hyperlink to connect data in your workbook to another document on your computer, network, corporate intranet or the Internet.

An intranet is a small version of the Internet within a company or organization.

CREATE A HYPERLINK

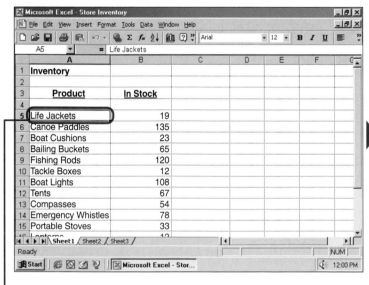

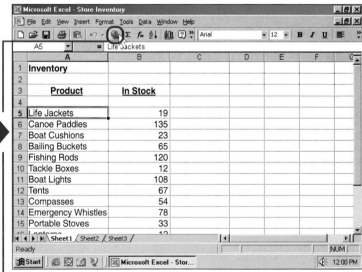

1 Select the cells containing the data you want to make a hyperlink. To select cells, see page 12.

2 Click 🔲 to create a hyperlink.

Note: If 🔲 is not displayed, click » on the Standard toolbar to display all the buttons.

■ The Insert Hyperlink dialog box appears.

Can I make a graphic a hyperlink?

Yes. If your workbook contains a graphic, such as an AutoShape or text effect, you can make the graphic a hyperlink. To make a graphic a hyperlink, click the graphic and then perform steps **2** to **7**, starting on page 210.

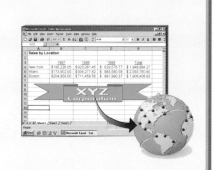

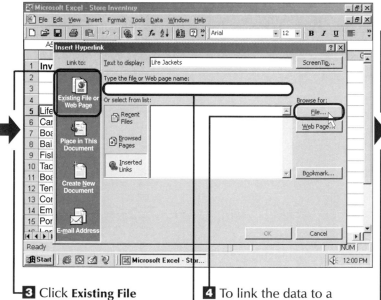

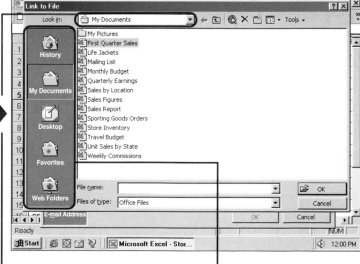

3 Click **Existing File or Web Page** to link the data to an existing document.

4 To link the data to a document on your computer or network, click **File**.

■ To link the data to a page on the Web, click this area and then type the address of the Web page (example: www.maran.com). Then skip to step **7** on page 212.

■ The Link to File dialog box appears.

■ This area shows the location of the displayed documents. You can click this area to change the location.

■ This area allows you to access commonly used folders. To display the contents of a folder, click the folder.

Note: For information on the commonly used folders, see the top of page 29.

CONTINUED ▶

CREATE A HYPERLINK

You can easily identify hyperlinks in your workbook. Hyperlinks appear underlined and in color.

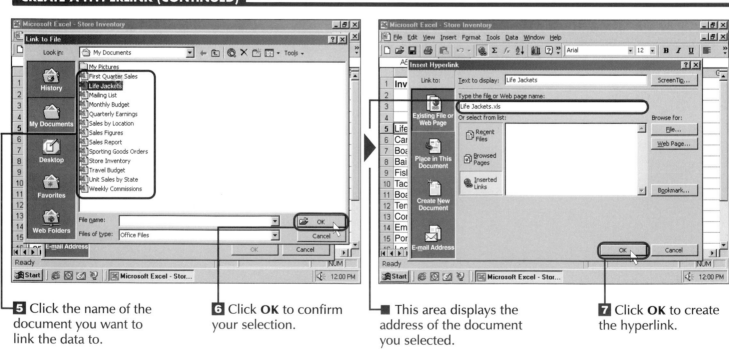

5 Click the name of the document you want to link the data to.

6 Click **OK** to confirm your selection.

■ This area displays the address of the document you selected.

7 Click **OK** to create the hyperlink.

TIP

**Can Excel automatically
create a hyperlink for me?**

When you type the address
of a document located on
your network or the Internet,
Excel will automatically
change the address to a
hyperlink for you.

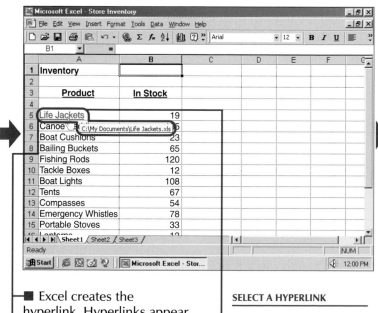

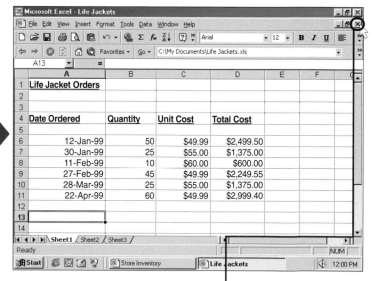

■ Excel creates the
hyperlink. Hyperlinks appear
underlined and in color.

■ When you position
the mouse 🖑 over the
hyperlink, a yellow box
appears, displaying where
the hyperlink will take you.

SELECT A HYPERLINK

1 Click a hyperlink to
display the document
or Web page connected
to the hyperlink.

■ The document or Web
page connected to the
hyperlink appears.

■ If the hyperlink connects
to a Web page, your Web
browser will open and
display the page.

2 When you finish
reviewing the document
or Web page, click ⊠
to close the window.

PREVIEW A WORKBOOK AS A WEB PAGE

You can preview how your workbook will look as a Web page. This allows you to see how the workbook will appear on the Internet or your company's intranet.

An intranet is a small version of the Internet within a company or organization.

PREVIEW A WORKBOOK AS A WEB PAGE

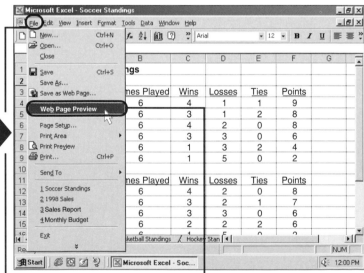

1 Open the workbook you want to preview as a Web page. To open a workbook, see page 34.

2 Click **File**.

3 Click **Web Page Preview** to preview your workbook as a Web page.

214

TIP

Will my Web page look the same to everyone who views the Web page?

No. Different Web browsers may display your Web page differently. Many Web browsers are used on the Web. The two most popular Web browsers are Microsoft Internet Explorer and Netscape Navigator.

Microsoft Internet Explorer

Netscape Navigator

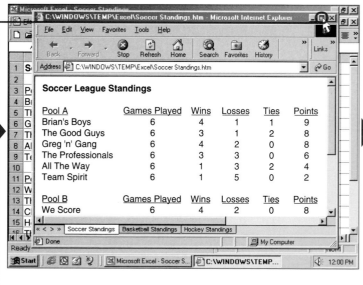

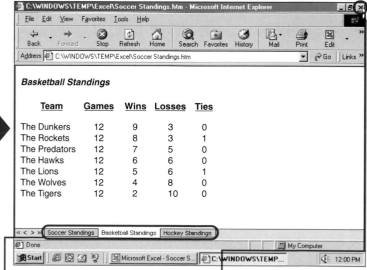

■ Your Web browser window opens, displaying your workbook as a Web page.

4 To maximize the Web browser window to fill your screen, click 🔲.

■ The gridlines that separate each cell do not appear in the Web browser window.

■ If your workbook contains more than one worksheet, this area displays a tab for each worksheet.

5 To display the contents of a different worksheet, click a tab.

6 When you finish reviewing your workbook as a Web page, click ✖ to close the Web browser window.

SAVE A WORKBOOK AS A WEB PAGE

You can save a workbook as a Web page. This lets you place the workbook on the Internet or your company's intranet.

An intranet is a small version of the Internet within a company or organization.

SAVE A WORKBOOK AS A WEB PAGE

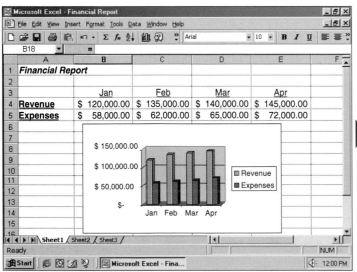

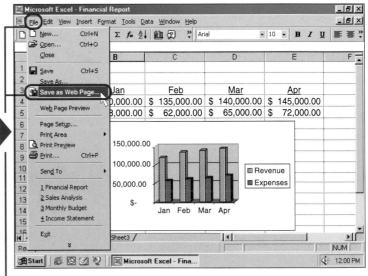

1 Open the workbook you want to save as a Web page. To open a workbook, see page 34.

2 Click **File**.

3 Click **Save as Web Page**.

■ The Save As dialog box appears.

216

How do I make my Web page available for other people to view?

After you save your workbook as a Web page, you can transfer the page to a computer that stores Web pages, called a Web server. Once you publish the Web page on a Web server, the page will be available for other people to view. For more information on publishing a Web page, contact your network administrator or Internet service provider.

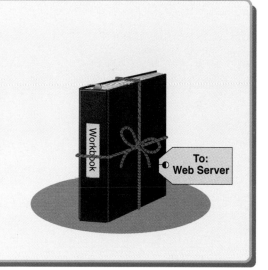

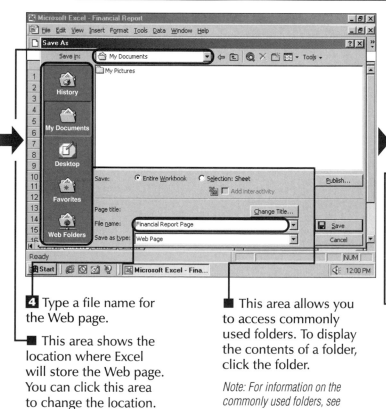

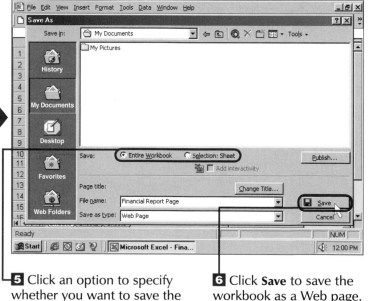

4 Type a file name for the Web page.

■ This area shows the location where Excel will store the Web page. You can click this area to change the location.

■ This area allows you to access commonly used folders. To display the contents of a folder, click the folder.

Note: For information on the commonly used folders, see the top of page 29.

5 Click an option to specify whether you want to save the entire workbook or just the current worksheet as a Web page (○ changes to ⊙).

6 Click **Save** to save the workbook as a Web page.

INDEX

NUMBERS & SYMBOLS

(error message), 82, 115
#DIV/0! (error message), 82
#NAME? (error message), 83
#REF! (error message), 59, 83
#VALUE! (error message), 83
$ (dollar sign), in absolute cell references, 81
( ) (parentheses)
    in formulas, 64
    in functions, 68
, (comma), in functions, 68
; (colon), in functions, 68
= (equal sign)
    in formulas, 64
    in functions, 68
3-D effects, add to graphics, 189

A

absolute references, 80-81
active cell
    change, 9
    overview, 8
add numbers, 76-77
addition. See formulas; functions
align. See also indent; rotate
    data, 103
area charts, 163
AutoCalculate feature, use, 74-75
AutoComplete feature, use, 11
AutoFilter feature
    turn off, 199
    use, 198-199, 200-201
AutoFormats
    apply, 124-125
    remove, 125
AutoShapes, add, 180-181
Average
    automatic calculation, 75
    function, 69

B

bar charts, 163
black and white, print in, 139
blue words in Help window, 25
bold data, 102, 104-107
borders, add, 110

browse through. See also scroll through
    worksheet tabs, 151
buttons, toolbar
    copy data using, 48-49
    display, 20
    move data using, 48-49

C

calculations. See formulas; functions
cancel changes, 45
category axis titles, in charts, 162, 165
cell references
    absolute, 80-81
    in formulas, 64
    overview, 8, 9
    relative, 78-79
cells
    active
        change, 9
        overview, 8
    AutoFormats, apply, 124-125
    borders, add, 110
    color, change, 108
    delete data from, 44
    deselect, 12
    display data vertically, 121
    edit data in, 42-43
    formatting
        copy, 122-123
        remove, 111
    name, 60-61
    overview, 8
    replace data in, 43
    rotate data in, 120-121
    select, 12-13
        named, 61
    wrap text in, 118-119
center data
    across columns, 117
    in cell, 103
    on page, 134
changes
    save, 29
    undo, 45
characters. See data; text
chart sheets, 166
Chart toolbar, 167
    display or hide, 21
Chart Wizard, 164-167

charts
    add data, 176-177
    create, 164-167
        using subtotals in lists, 205
    data series, 162
    delete, 167
        data, 177
    legends, 162
    move, 168
    overview, 5, 162-163
    parts of, 162
    plot style of data, change, 175
    preview, 171
    print, 170-171
    size, 168-169
    titles, 162, 165
        change, 174
    types, 163
        change, 172-173
check spelling, 50-51
circular reference, error in formulas, 83
clear
    formatting, 111
    print area, 133
click, using mouse, 6
Clipboard toolbar
    display or hide, 21
    use, 49
close
    Excel, 33
    workbooks, 32
color, change
    cells, 108-109
    data, 104-107, 108-109
    graphics, 188
column charts, 163
column labels in lists, 193
columns
    center data across, 117
    delete, 58-59
    display hidden, 89
    freeze, 92-93
    headings, print, 139
    hide, 88-89
    insert, 56-57
    labels, repeat on printed pages, 146-147
    overview, 8
    plot data by, in charts, 175
    select, 13
    unfreeze, 93
    width, change, 98

Comma format, 112
commands, select
    using menus, 18-19
    using toolbars, 20
conditions, specify for search, 36-39
copy
    data
        between worksheets, 156-157
        using drag and drop, 46-47
        using toolbar buttons, 48-49
    formatting, 122-123
    formulas
        using absolute references, 80-81
        using relative references, 78-79
    vs. move, 47, 157
correct spelling errors, 50-51
Count
    automatic calculation, 75
    function, 69
Count Nums, automatic calculation, 75
create
    charts, 164-167
        using subtotals in lists, 205
    hyperlinks, 210-213
    lists, 192-193
    workbooks, 30
Currency format, 112

D

data. See also records; text
    add to charts, 176-177
    align, 103
    appearance, change, 104-107
    bold, 102, 104-107
    center
        across columns, 117
        in cell, 103
        on page, 134
    color, change, 104-107, 108-109
    compare in lists, 200-201
    copy
        between worksheets, 156-157
        using drag and drop, 46-47
        using toolbar buttons, 48-49
    delete, 44
        from charts, 177
    display vertically in cells, 121
    edit, 42-43
        overview, 4
    effects, add, 104-107

enter, 10-11
  overview, 4
filter in lists, 198-199, 200-201
find, 52-53
font, change, 100
formatting, copy, 122-123
indent, 116
italicize, 102, 104-107
left align, 103
move
  between worksheets, 156-157
  using drag and drop, 46-47
  using toolbar buttons, 48-49
plot style, change, in charts, 175
printed, size, change, 144-145
replace
  in cells, 43
  using Replace feature, 54-55
right align, 103
rotate in cells, 120-121
save, 28-29
  as Web pages, 216-217
size, change, 101, 104-107
sort, in lists, 194-197
style, change, 102, 104-107
subtotaled, display or hide, 204
summarize, in lists, 202-203
underline, 102, 104-107
undo changes, 45
data forms, use to add records to lists, 192-193
data series
  in charts, 162
  complete, 14-15
decimal places, add or remove, 113, 114-115
delete. See also remove
  AutoShapes, 181
  borders, 110
  charts, 167
  columns, 58-59
  data, 44
    from charts, 177
  page breaks, 141
  rows, 58-59
  subtotals from lists, 205
  text boxes, 185
  text effects, 183
  worksheets, 153
deselect cells, 12
Desktop folder, 29
dialog boxes, move, 53, 71, 147

display. See also preview; view
  columns, hidden, 89
  data vertically in cells, 121
  Drawing toolbar, 21, 180
  full screen, 86
  menu commands, 18-19
  names of toolbar buttons, 20
  Office Assistant, 24
  records, hidden in lists, 199
  rows, hidden, 91
  subtotaled data, 204
  toolbar buttons, 20
  toolbars, 21
  worksheets, in Print Preview window, 128-129, 136
division. See formulas; functions
double-click, using mouse, 6
doughnut charts, 163
draft quality, print, 139
drag, using mouse, 6
drag and drop, use to move or copy data, 46-47
Drawing toolbar
  display, 21, 180
  hide, 21, 181

E

edit
  data, 42-43
    overview, 4
  formulas, 67
  text, in text boxes, 185
  text effects, 183
effects
  3-D, add to graphics, 189
  add to data, 104-107
  text, add, 182-183
electronic mail. See e-mail
e-mail
  workbooks, 209
  worksheets, 208-209
enlarge. See size; zoom
enter
  data, 10-11
    overview, 4
  formulas, 66-67
    across worksheets, 158-159
  functions, 70-73
errors
  in formulas, 82-83
  spelling, check for, 50-51

Excel. *See also specific subject or feature*
    documents. *See* workbooks; worksheets
    exit, 33
    and Internet, overview, 5
    overview, 4-5
    parts of screen, 8
    start, 7
exit. *See also* close
    Excel, 33

F

Favorites folder, 29
files, Excel. *See* workbooks; worksheets
filter lists, 198-199, 200-201
find
    data, 52-53
    workbooks, 36-39
FindFast feature, 39
folders, 29
fonts
    available in Excel, 105
    data, change, 100, 104-107
    size, change, 101, 104-107
footers
    add, 142-143
    remove, 143
format
    numbers, 112-113, 114-115
    worksheets, overview, 4
formatting
    clear, 111
    copy, 122-123
Formatting toolbar, 8
    display or hide, 21
forms, data, use to add records to lists, 192-193
formula bar, 8
formulas. *See also* functions
    copy
        using absolute references, 80-81
        using relative references, 78-79
    edit, 67
    enter, 66-67
        across worksheets, 158-159
    errors in, 82-83
    examples, 65
    find and replace numbers in, 55
    overview, 4, 64-65
freeze rows and columns, 92-93
full screen, display, 86

functions. *See also* formulas
    enter, 70-73
    examples, 69
    overview, 4, 68-69

G

graphics
    3-D effects, add, 189
    AutoShapes, 180-181
    color, change, 188
    make into hyperlinks, 211
    move, 186
    overview, 5
    size, 186-187
    text boxes, 184-185
    text effects, 182-183
gridlines, print, 139

H

handles
    around charts, 169
    around graphics, 187
headers
    add, 142-143
    remove, 143
height, of rows, change, 99
help, 24-25
hide
    columns, 88-89
    Drawing toolbar, 21, 181
    Office Assistant, 25
    parts of Excel screen, 86
    rows, 90-91
    subtotaled data, 204
    toolbars, 21
History folder, 29
hyperlinks
    create, 210-213
    select, 213
    use graphics as, 211

I

images. *See* graphics
indent data, 116
insert
    columns, 56-57
    data, 10-11, 42-43
    page breaks, 140-141
    rows, 56-57
    worksheets, new, 152

insertion point, move, 42, 67
Internet
    e-mail worksheets, 208-209
    hyperlinks
        create, 210-213
            using graphics, 211
        select, 213
    overview, 5
    Web pages
        preview workbooks as, 214-215
        save workbooks as, 216-217
intranets, 210, 214, 216
italicize data, 102, 104-107

K

keyboards, use number keys on right side, 43

L

labels
    column, in lists, 193
    repeat on printed pages, 146-147
landscape orientation, 135
left align data, 103
legends, in charts, 162
line charts, 163
lists
    compare data, 200-201
    create, 192-193
    filter, 198-199, 200-201
    overview, 5
    records, add, 192-193
    sort data, 194-197
    subtotals, 202-205

M

magnify. *See also* zoom setting
    pages, in Print Preview window, 129
margins
    center data between, 134
    change, 136-137
Max
    automatic calculation, 75
    function, 69
menu bar, 8
menus, select commands using, 18-19
messages, e-mail, send worksheets as, 208-209
Microsoft Excel. *See* Excel

Min
    automatic calculation, 75
    function, 69
mouse
    use, 6
    wheeled, 17
move
    between worksheets, 150-151
    charts, 168
    data
        between worksheets, 156-157
        using drag and drop, 46-47
        using toolbar buttons, 48-49
    dialog boxes, 53, 71, 147
    graphics, 186
    insertion point, 42, 67
    through worksheets, 16-17
    toolbars, 23
    vs. copy, 47, 157
    worksheets, 155
multiplication. *See* formulas; functions
My Documents folder, 29

N

name
    cells, 60-61
    workbooks, 28-29
named cells, select, 61
names of toolbar buttons, display, 20
NUM display, turn on or off, 43
number keys on right side of keyboard, use, 43
number series
    complete, 14-15
    vs. text series, 15
numbers. *See also* data; records; text
    add, 76-77
    decimal places, add or remove, 113
    format, 112-113
        using Format Cells dialog box, 114-115
    formatting, copy, 122-123
    insert, using number keys on right side of keyboard, 43
    styles, change, 112, 114-115

O

Office Assistant
    display, 24
    get help using, 24-25
    hide, 25
    welcome, 7

open
    Excel, 7
    workbooks, 34-35
orientation, pages, change, 135

P

page breaks
    delete, 141
    insert, 140-141
pages. *See also* worksheets
    center data on, 134
    headers and footers, add, 142-143
    magnify in Print Preview window, 129
    margins, change, 136-137
    orientation, change, 135
    printed, repeat labels on, 146-147
    Web
        preview workbooks as, 214-215
        save workbooks as, 216-217
Percent format, 112
pictures. *See* graphics
pie charts, 163
plot style of data, change, in charts, 175
point sizes, 101. *See also* fonts
portrait orientation, 135
preview. *See also* display; view
    charts, using Print Preview feature, 171
    workbooks, as Web pages, 214-215
    worksheets, 128-129
print
    area, 132-133
    charts, 170-171
    options, change, 138-139
    worksheets, 130-131
        overview, 5
Print Preview feature, use, 128-129
printed
    data, size, change, 144-145
    pages, repeat labels on, 146-147
properties, specify for search, 36-39

R

radar charts, 163
records. *See also* data; text
    add to lists, 192-193
    filter, 198-199, 200-201
    overview, 193
    redisplay, in lists, 199
    sort, 194-197
reduce. *See* size; zoom

references
    absolute, 80-81
    cell, 8, 9
        in formulas, 64
    relative, 78-79
relative references, 78-79
remove. *See also* delete
    3-D effects from graphics, 189
    AutoFormats, 125
    bold from data, 102
    borders, 110
    color
        from cells, 108
        from data, 109
        from graphics, 188
    data, 44
        from charts, 177
    decimal places, 113, 114-115
    footers, 143
    formatting, 111
    headers, 143
    indent, 116
    italics from data, 102
    page breaks, 141
    split from worksheets, 95
    subtotals, 205
    underlines from data, 102
    worksheets, 153
rename. *See also* name
    worksheets, 154
replace data
    in cells, 43
    using Replace feature, 54-55
resize. *See* size
right align data, 103
right-click, using mouse, 6
rotate data in cells, 120-121
Round, function, 69
rows
    delete, 58-59
    display hidden, 91
    freeze, 92-93
    headings, print, 139
    height, change, 99
    hide, 90-91
    insert, 56-57
    labels, repeat on printed pages, 146-147
    overview, 8
    plot data by, in charts, 175
    select, 13
    unfreeze, 93

S

save, workbooks, 28-29
    as Web pages, 216-217
screens
    display full, 86
    Excel, parts of, 8
scroll through. *See also* browse through
    worksheets, 16-17
search. *See* find
select
    cells, 12-13
    columns, 13
    commands
        using menus, 18-19
        using toolbars, 20
    hyperlinks, 213
    named cells, 61
    rows, 13
series
    complete, 14-15
    data, in charts, 162
shapes, add, 180-181
size
    charts, 168-169
    data, 101, 104-107
    graphics, 186-187
    printed data, 144-145
    text, to fit in cells, 119
    toolbars, 22
sort data in lists, 194-197
spelling, check, 50-51
split worksheets, 94-95
spreadsheets. *See* Excel; worksheets
Standard toolbar, 8
    display or hide, 21
start. *See also* open
    Excel, 7
strikethrough effect, 107
style
    of data, change, 102, 104-107
    of numbers, change, 112, 114-115
subscript effect, 107
subtotaled data, display or hide, 204
subtotals in lists, 202-205
subtraction. *See* formulas; functions
Sum
    automatic calculation, 75
    function, 69

sum of numbers, calculate, 76-77
summarize data in lists, 202-203
superscript effect, 107
switch between
    workbooks, 31
    worksheets, 150-151

T

tabs, worksheet, 8
    browse through, 151
taskbar, switch between workbooks using, 31
text. *See also* data; records
    add to AutoShapes, 181
    edit, in text boxes, 185
    series
        complete, 14-15
        vs. number series, 15
    shrink to fit in cells, 119
    wrap in cells, 118-119
text boxes, 184-185
text effects, 182-183
titles
    add to charts, 164-165
    of charts, change, 174
toolbars
    buttons
        copy data using, 48-49
        display, 20
            names, 20
        move data using, 48-49
    Chart, 167
    Clipboard, use, 49
    display, 21
    Drawing
        display, 21, 180
        hide, 21, 181
    hide, 21
    move, 23
    select commands using, 20
    size, 22
turn off AutoFilter feature, 199
types of charts, change, 172-173

U

underline data, 102, 104-107
undo changes, 45
unfreeze rows or columns, 93

V

value axis titles, in charts, 162, 165
values, specify for search, 36-39
view. *See also* display; preview
    footers, 142-143
    headers, 142-143
    repeated labels, using Print Preview feature, 147

W

Web Folders folder, 29
Web pages
    preview workbooks as, 214-215
    save workbooks as, 216-217
Web servers, 217
wheeled mouse, scroll through worksheets using, 17
width of columns, change, 98
WordArt feature, use, 182-183
words, blue, in Help window, 25
workbooks. *See also* Excel; worksheets
    close, 32
    create, 30
    delete worksheets from, 153
    e-mail, 209
    find, 36-39
    insert worksheets, 152
    open, 34-35
    overview, 8
    preview as Web pages, 214-215
    print, 130-131
    save, 28-29
      as Web pages, 216-217
    switch between, 31
worksheet tabs, 8
    browse through, 151
worksheets. *See also* cells; columns; data; Excel; pages;
 rows; workbooks
    check spelling, 50-51
    data
      copy between, 156-157
      enter, 10-11
      find, 52-53
      move between, 156-157
    delete, 153
    display full screen, 86
    e-mail, 208-209
    enter formulas across, 158-159
    footers, add, 142-143

    format, overview, 4
    headers, add, 142-143
    insert new, 152
    margins, change, 136-137
    move, 155
    overview, 8
    preview, 128-129
    print, 130-131
      options, change, 138-139
      overview, 5
    print area, set, 132-133
    remove formatting, 111
    remove split, 95
    rename, 154
    scroll through, 16-17
    select all cells, 13
    split, 94-95
    switch between, 150-151
    zoom setting, change, 87
wrap text in cells, 118-119

X

xy (scatter) charts, 163

Z

zoom setting, change, 87

OVER 6 MILLION

OTHER 3-D Visual SERIES

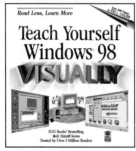

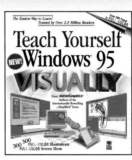

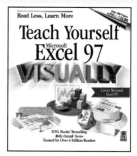

IDG BOOKS ®

TRADE & INDIVIDUAL ORDERS

Phone: **(800) 762-2974**
or **(317) 596-5200**
(8 a.m.–6 p.m., CST, weekdays)
FAX : **(800) 550-2747**
or **(317) 596-5692**

EDUCATIONAL ORDERS & DISCOUNTS

Phone: **(800) 434-2086**
(8:30 a.m.–5:00 p.m., CST, weekdays)
FAX : **(317) 596-5499**

CORPORATE ORDERS FOR 3-D VISUAL™ SERIES

Phone: **(800) 469-6616**
(8 a.m.–5 p.m., EST, weekdays)
FAX : **(905) 890-9434**

Qty	ISBN	Title	Price	Total

Shipping & Handling Charges

	Description	First book	Each add'l. book	Total
Domestic	Normal	$4.50	$1.50	$
	Two Day Air	$8.50	$2.50	$
	Overnight	$18.00	$3.00	$
International	Surface	$8.00	$8.00	$
	Airmail	$16.00	$16.00	$
	DHL Air	$17.00	$17.00	$

Subtotal _____

*CA residents add
applicable sales tax* _____

*IN, MA and MD
residents add
5% sales tax* _____

*IL residents add
6.25% sales tax* _____

*RI residents add
7% sales tax* _____

*TX residents add
8.25% sales tax* _____

Shipping _____

Total _____

Ship to:

Name _____

Address _____

Company _____

City/State/Zip _____

Daytime Phone _____

Payment: □ Check to IDG Books (US Funds Only)
□ Visa □ Mastercard □ American Express

Card # _____ Exp. _____ Signature _____

maranGraphics™